Mysterious Disappearance of Mr. Darcy

KELLY MILLER

THE MYSTERIOUS DISAPPEARANCE
OF MR. DARCY

ISBN: 979-8-9879813-2-0

Cover design by Pemberley Darcy using stock images
Edited by Jo Abbott
Edited by Carol S. Bowes
Book layout by Suzanne Minae

Published in the United States of America.

A Note

SPELLING AND LANGUAGE IN THE MYSTERIOUS DISAPPEARANCE OF MR. DARCY

In order to bring authenticity to the time frame and setting of this story, the Regency era in England, an effort was made to avoid including any phrases, words, or word usages that would not have existed in 1811 England. Also, British English spellings and word usages were utilized even though the author's own familiarity is with American English. For instance, "turn round" is used rather than "turn around." In addition, the author followed traditional British usage for should/would and shall/will.

To my wonderful mom,
Thank you so much for everything!

CHAPTER 1

The Disagreeable Stranger

Saturday, 3 August 1811
Ramsgate
Elizabeth Bennet

I LEANED OVER MY RIGHT FOOT, ARCHED MY ARM BACK, and cast Rory's ball across the beach. My collie raced in pursuit of the toy. His joyful barks superseded the drone of the waves and the seagulls' calls. His brown-and-white fur, soaking wet from the seawater, lay flat against his skin, lending him a more diminutive appearance than usual.

With a long, slow inhalation, I savoured the damp, salty air and marvelled at the graceful dance of the tide. How could anyone fail to be fascinated by the seaside?

Rory scampered back to me, dropped the ball, and waited with his ears straight up, his body taut, his weight over his haunches.

"Are you ready, boy?" I tossed the ball again, this time farther from the water, and Rory raced away after it. But rather than return the toy to me, he veered off towards a pretty, young blonde lady seated alone on a blanket. I stiffened. *Oh no, Rory—not this again!* My sweet collie did not comprehend that not everyone loved dogs—some feared or even hated them. Would this stranger be annoyed by his intrusion?

It appeared not, for the young lady displayed a bright, cheery countenance, and she reached out to stroke Rory, despite his sandy, damp state.

I drew closer to them. "Pardon me, but I hope my dog is not bothering you. He has a bad habit of soliciting strangers to join in his favourite game."

"No, I do not mind at all. I am fond of dogs." Her soft voice impelled me to step nearer. She picked up the ball. "What game is that?"

"Rory loves to fetch-and-carry."

"Oh, that is charming. So his name is Rory—it fits him." She raised the ball, and my dog leaned back on his hind legs, his eyes on the toy. "If I throw this, will he bring it back to me?"

"Yes, he will play all day with a willing participant."

"May I try?"

"By all means."

She rose to her feet and flung the ball, giggling when Rory shot off in pursuit. He retrieved his quarry and dropped it before her again. "You are a clever one." Her blue eyes gleamed as she picked up the toy. "He is beautiful too. I have never seen a prettier dog."

"Thank you. You ought to see him when he is clean and dry. At present, his coat is—"

"What is going on here?"

I recoiled and whirled towards the hostile voice. A well-dressed, tall gentleman—a dark-haired Adonis with an exceptional figure—strode towards us holding two cups of lemonade from one of the vendors. *My goodness, what a handsome man!* But his distinct sneer spoilt his otherwise captivating person. Rory darted into the space between us and released a guttural growl.

"Fitzwilliam, all is well." The young lady directed a forced smile at the man. "I have been speaking to this kind lady. Her dog brought his ball to me." She held the toy up before him.

"I see." The gentleman's piercing dark eyes narrowed when they settled upon me. His mien conveyed disdain, the way one might regard an annoying insect.

Who did he think he was? I conquered the inclination to shrink from him and set my shoulders back. "My collie is obedient on most occasions, but he is not well-versed in etiquette. It is not my habit to accost anyone without a prior introduction, but I wanted to ensure my dog did not distress the young lady."

He folded his arms across his chest. "Well, you contrived a novel approach at least. Nevertheless, you have wasted your time."

"I do not take your meaning."

"You may dispense with the pretence now, for your ruse has failed. You are not the first to attempt to attract my notice through my sister."

My mouth fell open. "Attract *your* notice? I have never heard anything so arrogant! You must suffer from an inflated sense of self-importance. I have no idea who you are, and I do not care to know. Furthermore, I pity you."

His nostrils flared. No doubt few people dared to address him in such an unguarded way, but I had seldom encountered anyone more deserving of a set-down.

I turned to the young lady, who wore a stricken expression. "I apologise for my unpleasantness just now. I enjoyed our conversation, and I wish *you* a good day." I spun on my heel and marched off, only to make an abrupt halt. *Darn,* I could not leave without Rory's ball. Without a glimpse in the gentleman's direction, I turned and retraced my steps to the young lady, who handed the toy to me. I departed again with Rory trotting at my side.

At the house, I utilised the servants' entrance and passed Rory's leash to Peggy, a maid of the household. "I am afraid he needs another bath."

"That's to be expected, miss. This one's no trouble to bathe. 'E doesn't fight me any. 'E seems to like it."

I gave Rory's head a pat. "Yes, he loves the water."

An hour later, I joined my aunt Modesty Gardiner and Mrs. Rebecca Stapleton for breakfast. The spacious dining-parlour featured a large window with a splendid view of the sea. Mrs. Stapleton, a wealthy widow in her sixth decade and a dear friend of Aunt Gardiner's, had purchased this seaside home earlier in the year and invited Aunt Gardiner and me to stay for the month of August.

"Did you enjoy your walk, Lizzy?" My aunt, a personable, petite lady of two-and-thirty, rapped her boiled egg with a spoon.

I swallowed a mouthful of ham. "It was wonderful. A walk along the seashore is such a treat. I spied a pair of dolphins leaping out of the water this morning."

"They are fascinating creatures." Mrs. Stapleton's pale blue eyes glittered.

"Rory enjoyed himself too. He made a game out of chasing the outgoing waves and running from the incoming ones. When he grew weary of that, I threw his ball for him."

"Your dog certainly loves to play." Mrs. Stapleton poured a cup of tea and shifted her plump figure forwards to hold out the beverage. "Here you are."

"Thank you." I accepted the cup and took a sip. "Towards the end of my walk, I…um…had an unpleasant encounter with a gentleman."

"Oh?" Aunt Gardiner stirred sugar into her tea. "Did Rory shake his fur next to the man and get him wet?"

"No, nothing like that occurred, but Rory played a part in the incident. He approached the gentleman's sister while she sat alone on the beach. I shared a brief conversation with the young lady and found her to be cordial. She took delight in Rory—until the gentleman appeared. He made it obvious my presence was unwelcome. He even accused me of having schemed to meet *him* through his sister! I had never before witnessed such conceit."

My aunt's lips drew flat. "It is a shame that man put a damper on your otherwise agreeable walk. I presume he is a pampered, affluent denizen of the *ton* who is accustomed to attracting attention wherever he goes. I have witnessed more than my share of similar haughty conduct in London."

"Do not fret, my dear." Mrs. Stapleton moved the toast rack

closer to me. "I have met most of my neighbours, and but for one or two, they are genial and kind. I shall ensure you meet the best of them during your stay. Pray, do not allow one rotten apple to spoil your impression of Ramsgate."

"Oh no, I shall not. I have already forgotten the man."

"Good for you." My aunt beamed at me.

I responded with a blithe smile. But to my chagrin, the moment I had spoken the words, a vivid image of the exasperating—and oh-so-attractive—gentleman burst to the forefront of my mind, disrupting my peace. Well, he would *soon* be forgotten.

Monday, 5 August
Stapleton House, Ramsgate

At the knock upon the front door, Mrs. Stapleton stirred from her relaxed position, her hands fluttering. "Goodness me, I had meant to mention earlier that we shall have guests for dinner—my neighbours at the east end of the street."

My aunt adopted a cheerful air. "That is a pleasant surprise. I am eager to meet them."

"I am as well." I duplicated my aunt's merry tone. Yesterday, we had tea at the home of a neighbour. Our hosts, an affable couple of a similar age to Mrs. Stapleton, could not have been kinder.

The butler appeared at the door to the drawing-room. "Mr. and Miss Darcy, madam." A well-dressed, dark-haired gentleman and a tall, blonde lady entered.

I froze. It was *them*—the vain fool from the beach and his amiable sister. The gentleman, Mr. Darcy, gave Mrs. Stapleton a cordial greeting and had not yet noticed me. Darned if he did not appear even more alluring tonight than he had on Saturday morning, when a scowl had distorted his well-favoured face. He made such a captivating picture that, to my dismay, it took an effort to prise my eyes from him. I stood by, fidgeting with my gloves, as Mrs. Stapleton introduced the pair to my aunt.

Aunt Gardiner stammered through her greeting to the gentleman. I had never witnessed my sensible, self-confident aunt in such a flustered state. What explained her odd response to Mr. Darcy?

Then Miss Darcy gazed in my direction and started, her azure eyes widening. A moment later, her lips edged upwards.

Mrs. Stapleton gestured to me. "Miss Bennet, I should like you to meet Miss Darcy and Mr. Darcy of Pemberley estate in Derbyshire." He turned to me, and his forward movement faltered, but he made a swift recovery.

"And this is Mrs. Gardiner's niece, Miss Elizabeth Bennet of Longbourn estate in Hertfordshire."

I rose from my curtsey and fixed upon the blonde young lady. "I am pleased to see you again, Miss Darcy."

"I am glad to know your name, Miss Bennet, and happy to meet you here. What a coincidence to find we are neighbours!"

Mr. Darcy bowed, his dark eyes probing me. "It is a pleasure to meet you, Miss Bennet."

Clearly, he could be polite when it suited him. I offered a near smile. "And you, Mr. Darcy."

Mrs. Stapleton's sight settled upon me. "Ah, it seems you and the

Darcys have been in company before." Aunt Gardiner, who had regained her former composure, looked on as well.

My stomach contracted. "Yes...ah...on the beach the other morning, Rory took his ball to Miss Darcy."

"Oh, *I see.*" Mrs. Stapleton's lips quirked to the side.

"When did you arrive in Ramsgate?" Miss Darcy came closer to me.

"On Thursday. How long have you been here?"

"Since the first week in June."

I queried Miss Darcy on her favourite places in and around town, and she described several shops, the concert hall, and a public garden.

During a pause in our conversation, Mr. Darcy moved his tall, robust form next to his sister. "Miss Bennet, I apologise for my insolence the other day. I had no justification for the cursory assumption I made."

I raised my eyes to him. He presented no sign of his former arrogance. "Your apology is accepted. I cannot defend my own actions on that occasion. In the past, my aunt has cautioned me to be more disciplined in my speech."

"In consideration of the way I had provoked you, your response was understandable. In actuality, I am glad you spoke your mind—I deserved no less." His weight shifted to his heels. "Although, I am puzzled by a statement you made that day."

"What is that?"

"Why did you say you *pitied* me?" His handsome features constricted.

A wave of heat circulated over my countenance. I twisted to obtain a glimpse of my aunt and Mrs. Stapleton, who still observed us. "At the time, I blurted the words without forethought. But I suppose I said it because anyone who demonstrates ungentlemanly conduct to a stranger in public must not comprehend the importance of kindness and treating others with respect, and that is rather...pathetic."

"I am touched to the quick." He spoke under his breath.

"Forgive me, I ought to have tempered my response. I did not intend to offend you."

"No, you need not apologise. I asked you for an explanation, and mortifying as it may be, I prefer to hear the truth. Despite all evidence to the contrary, I do know better, and I shall take care to improve my behaviour in the future."

Devoid of a response, I stared at him. I should never have expected my words to make the least impression upon him. To my good fortune, Mrs. Stapleton covered for my mute state: she approached Mr. Darcy and raised the subject of a mutual acquaintance recovering from an illness. Miss Darcy and I resumed our conversation regarding Ramsgate and the surrounding towns.

At dinner, I sat beside Miss Darcy. I learnt she shared my love of music, and we enjoyed a protracted discussion of our favourite composers. Mr. Darcy, although engaged in dialogue by Mrs. Stapleton and my aunt, sent me frequent glances. He had yet to smile this evening, but at least he refrained from glaring.

Miss Darcy leaned close to me. "I should love to hear you play."

"I do not know what Mrs. Stapleton has planned for tonight, but if you like, I could ask her if we could perform after dinner. She has a fine array of music, so I am certain you will find a piece with which you are familiar."

"Oh no." Her blonde eyebrows drifted lower. "I have never played in front of strangers before." She fiddled with her gold bracelet. "Not that *you* are a stranger, but our acquaintance is new, and I just met your aunt."

"Still, if you want to practise performing for others, you would be hard-pressed to find a more amiable audience than my aunt and Mrs. Stapleton."

"No, I am not ready to perform—not tonight. Perhaps I shall on another occasion."

"As you wish."

"I wonder...ah...perhaps you might...um...like to have tea with me at my house tomorrow at one o'clock. I could show you my music, and perchance we could choose a duet to play together."

"That sounds delightful. I should like to come, but I must warn you not to expect too much from my playing. While you studied with a music master, I learnt to play and read music from my aunt Gardiner. In addition, my dedication to practice has been...erratic."

"That is of no consequence, I assure you." A sparkle enlivened Miss Darcy's eyes. "So, shall I see you tomorrow at one?"

"Yes, thank you." I sliced a bite-sized piece of beef, but my next thought tempered my appetite. I regarded Miss Darcy. "Are you certain your brother will approve of your invitation?"

"I cannot imagine why he would object." Miss Darcy's shoulders sank. "Albeit, I...um...have not always demonstrated the best judgment of late."

I touched her arm. "I suggest you seek your brother's opinion later tonight when the two of you are alone. If he raises any objection, you may send me a message to cancel. Otherwise, I shall arrive at one tomorrow as planned."

"Yes, that is a fine idea—I shall do that. You are very considerate." Miss Darcy grimaced. "I apologise, it is mortifying to be doubtful over anything so simple as an invitation to tea."

"You need not be embarrassed."

She presented a weak smile. "This is new to me. Since I am not yet out, I have had few opportunities to invite friends to my home."

"No matter what happens, I am honoured you asked me." When we returned to the drawing-room, Miss Darcy elected to sit beside me again. Mr. Darcy, my aunt, and Mrs. Stapleton sat opposite us.

Miss Darcy angled her head to view me. "It was delightful to meet Rory the other day. How old is he?"

"He is five years old. This is his first trip to the seaside, and he loves it here as much as I do."

Mrs. Stapleton handed Miss Darcy a fresh cup of tea. "If you would like to see Rory, we could have him brought here for a short time."

"Oh yes, it would be a treat to see him." Miss Darcy glanced at me. "If Miss Bennet does not mind."

"Not at all, and Rory will be pleased to meet you again."

"Yes, he will. The rascal loves attention." Mrs. Stapleton winked at Miss Darcy, then made her wishes known to a maid. A few minutes later, Peggy entered the room with Rory at her side.

"Oh, how sweet." Miss Darcy giggled. "He brought his ball."

"Rory, bring it here." My dog ran to me and dropped the toy. He turned to Miss Darcy and sniffed her legs, wagging his tail.

She reached out and patted him. "Do you remember me, Rory?"

In his evident enthusiasm, my dog's tail became fuzzy with movement—until he fixed on Mr. Darcy. Rory's attitude tensed, his ears shot back, and he emitted a soft growl.

"I am afraid I did not make a favourable first impression upon Rory." Mr. Darcy's complexion flushed.

"All is well, boy." I used a soothing tone. My dog ceased growling, but he kept Mr. Darcy in his sight, and his hind legs lowered, as though prepared to pounce if necessary.

"My brother has a way with dogs." A crease formed on Miss Darcy's forehead. "They almost always favour him."

Mr. Darcy rose from his seat and crouched upon the rug. He held a hand out to my collie. "Rory, my sister is right—you ought to grant me a second chance. I could name at least five dogs of my acquaintance who would vouch for my good character."

My attention riveted upon the dapper, proud Mr. Darcy on his knees in an attempt to allay Rory's disquiet. "You may want to try this." I tossed the ball to the gentleman, who caught it deftly in his palm.

"Thank you." Mr. Darcy bounced the ball and caught it again. Rory's ears perked up. "Well, old boy, let us see if I can persuade you to play." He held the ball out in front of Rory, then made an underhanded toss, sending the toy across the room.

Rory darted away in pursuit. He trotted back with it, coming to within five feet of Mr. Darcy, and wavered. My dog paused several seconds before he continued and dropped the ball before the gentleman.

Miss Darcy clapped her hands. "It worked, Fitzwilliam!"

"It seems I am forgiven." He threw the ball again, and this time

Rory returned it without hesitation. Mr. Darcy handed the ball to his sister. "I imagine you would like to play with him."

"Yes, I should." Mr. Darcy returned to his seat, and Miss Darcy indulged Rory in the game, throwing his toy several times. She stroked my dog's fur and glanced at me. "Does he do any other tricks?"

"Yes, he does—at least, he will if he is in the right mood. Let us find out." In response to my commands, Rory rolled over, bowed, and shook hands with Miss Darcy before Peggy took him from the room.

"Who is reading the John Locke essay?" Mr. Darcy pointed towards Papa's worn copy of *An Essay Concerning Human Understanding, Volume IV,* that I had left on a side table.

"I finished it this afternoon." His dark irises bored into me, and a concurrent rise in my body temperature spurred my blush.

"It has been a few years, but I read all four volumes. What did you think of them?"

An odd fluttering afflicted my belly, making me vacillate. Did he truly care to hear my opinion? I began my commentary in a tentative style. In time, buoyed by the conviction of my impressions and ideas, my speech grew more emphatic. I braced for Mr. Darcy to belittle my notions and treat me in the patronising way other men had before him. Instead, he debated me as one would an equal, the way my father did. And in doing so, he put forth salient, astute arguments that left me less secure in my beliefs and desirous of seeking his opinions on a myriad of other matters.

When our discussion reached its completion, Mrs. Stapleton suggested we take turns reading from a book of poetry. We spent a pleasant hour in that activity, which left me with a distinct preference for Mr. Darcy's sonorous baritone, before the Darcys took their leave.

No sooner had they departed when my aunt confronted our host. "Rebecca, how could you have neglected to mention we should spend the evening with one of London's most sought-after and illustrious bachelors?"

I swallowed. *Most sought-after and illustrious?* Could this be true?

Mrs. Stapleton waved her hand. "That is a bit of an exaggeration. Whilst Mr. Darcy receives more than his share of attention in London, he is not titled. Many ladies in the top tier of society will set their caps upon no one below a viscount."

"Yet his name is often in the gossip columns."

"It is not his fault if the authors of those frivolous articles seek the smallest crumbs of information they can find regarding him and speculate when they cannot uncover any. By all accounts, he is a responsible estate owner and an excellent guardian to his sister. I have known him for many years and have never observed anything in his demeanour to give me pause." Mrs. Stapleton veered towards me. "I presume Mr. Darcy is the man who made an unfavourable impression upon you the other morning."

"Yes. From our initial encounter, I should have deemed him incapable of contrition. However, his apology appeared to be genuine."

Mrs. Stapleton nodded. "I have no doubt he spoke in earnest, and it takes strength of character to admit one's mistakes."

"Nevertheless"—my aunt folded her arms—"I wish you had spoken to me before you invited him here."

"What troubles you, Modesty?" Mrs. Stapleton sat on the sofa and patted the area beside her.

Aunt Gardiner took the seat, resting her forearm on the edge of the sofa. "I...um...am hesitant to mention this with my niece present."

I sat in a chair opposite my aunt. "Please do not be concerned for my sake. You know I am not the least bit missish, and I shall be one-and-twenty on my next birthday. Besides, he is Mrs. Stapleton's neighbour, so in all likelihood, we shall cross paths again. After having spent time with him, I am eager to hear what you have to say."

"Very well. I shall skirt propriety on this occasion because I believe you are mature enough for this conversation." Vertical folds arose between my aunt's brows when she faced Mrs. Stapleton again. "Perhaps you have not seen all that has been written about Mr. Darcy. For instance, are you aware he has been observed in public with a well-known London actress, Miss Frances Comerford? Many believe she is, or was, his *mistress*."

I sucked in a quick breath. "Miss Comerford...why is that name familiar?" Moments later, an image came to me of the auburn-haired actress's beautiful visage.

Aunt Gardiner gave me an intent look. "We saw her last year in that farce at the Haymarket Theatre."

"I remember now—the stunning redhead?"

"Yes, that one."

Mrs. Stapleton shrugged. "I have heard the whispers too, but I urge you not to jump to conclusions. Many rumours are untrue."

My aunt frowned. "Yes, but this particular report has endured, and many of my friends believe it. So, while it may be embellished, it is apt to have a basis in fact."

"Perhaps there is a friendship between them, but it may not be a romantic one."

"What else have I read about him?" Aunt Gardiner's eyes narrowed. "Oh yes, now I remember—it is said he has frequented certain...unsavoury businesses."

I stilled, my every muscle tense. What did she mean? Gambling halls? *Bordellos?*

Mrs. Stapleton's lips twitched. "Ah, yes, now that you mention it, I have heard that too. I should not be surprised if that is true. After all, he has lacked a father's guidance these past five years. Young men often sow wild oats before they mature, marry, and take on other responsibilities."

Or maybe they formed habits they would be reluctant to give up, even after they married. A sudden chill prompted me to rub my bare forearms.

Mrs. Stapleton eyed me. "A close friend of mine, Mrs. Townshend, has known Mr. Darcy since his youth and has the highest opinion of him. She contends that *all* sordid deeds attributed to him are lies borne from jealousy and spite."

A yearning in my chest urged me to accept Mrs. Townshend's view of Mr. Darcy, but how could I when I did not even know the lady? In any case, it would not be fair to allow mere rumours to taint my opinion of him. I should judge him based upon my own observations.

"Your friend may be biased due to her long association with the Darcy family." Aunt Gardiner lowered her chin. "On the other hand, people often spread salacious tales without making any effort to determine their veracity."

"Yes, quite right." A jaunty pitch coloured Mrs. Stapleton's discourse. "Keep in mind that for the past several Seasons, new groups of ladies have attempted and failed to catch Mr. Darcy's notice. I have heard many of them lament their failure to attract him, and in their frustration, some are eager to disparage him. One such indiscreet lady shared her suspicion with me that his preference lies in another direction, if you take my meaning." Her features pinched. "Oh, do forgive me, Miss Bennet—I ought not to have been so frank."

Aunt Gardiner patted her friend's hand. "Do not fret. My niece is aware not all people are attracted to the opposite sex. The steward at Longbourn has maintained a close association with the head groom for years."

"Ah, well, I am relieved to know I did not shock her." Mrs. Stapleton smiled at me.

My aunt canted her head. "Maybe the lady's speculation is true. If Mr. Darcy's romantic predilection went towards males, he would prefer people believed he had a mistress rather than learnt the truth."

"No, it is not true." Mrs. Stapleton spoke with surety. "Before tonight, I might have entertained the possibility, but no longer."

"Why do you say, 'before tonight'?" Aunt Gardiner peered at Mrs. Stapleton. "And how could you be certain?"

"Because I noted the way he looked at Miss Bennet this evening in unguarded moments. In particular, I found the debate between them to be enlightening in more ways than one."

What could Mrs. Stapleton mean? I twisted the garnet cross on my necklace.

"Well, he admired Lizzy's arguments"—Aunt Gardiner gestured to me—"but he is not the first gentleman to be impressed by her intellect and creativeness."

"Oh yes, he did, but this went far beyond admiration. Your niece entranced him. He is smitten." Mrs. Stapleton grinned at me. "You may have the opportunity to make an extraordinary match."

My breath rushed out. "You flatter me, Mrs. Stapleton, but I am sure you are mistaken. From what you have said, Mr. Darcy can have his pick of ladies from society's top tier. He would have no reason to consider anyone like *me* as a potential spouse. That would defy logic."

"Matters of the heart are not logical, my dear."

The sweet lady meant well, but what a ridiculous suggestion! Now that she had given it voice, though, the notion absorbed me. For although I should have been loath to admit it, the mysterious, impressive, and fascinating Mr. Darcy had inspired a fanciful, hopeless longing. Nevertheless, a connexion between us could never happen. He had met my aunt, the most genteel, gracious, and knowledgeable of my relations. But if he met my mother or youngest sister... I could not picture it without cringing. "Even if you are correct, and he finds me attractive, it does not signify. Once he knows my family's situation, his interest in me will vanish."

"It pains me to say it, but my niece is correct." My aunt glanced my way. "All too often, people have altered their treatment of me upon learning my husband is a tradesman."

"Ah, but he already knows the pertinent details of your situation, and Miss Bennet's as well." Mrs. Stapleton reposed against the sofa with a canny smirk. "Before your arrival in Ramsgate, I sat beside Mr. Darcy at a dinner given by another neighbour and engaged him in conversation. I mentioned that I expected guests to arrive soon and described you both in detail."

"Why did you do that?" asked Aunt Gardiner.

"I wanted to determine his perspective. Mr. Darcy has a reputation for being proud, yet he has formed friendships with gentlemen whose wealth came from trade. If he had revealed the slightest hint of disapproval for either of you, I should not have invited him here during your stay."

Then he already knew my mother's side of the family came from trade! A sensation of lightness energised my limbs.

"Oh, I see." Aunt Gardiner relaxed against the sofa. "That is most thoughtful of you. But I should not want you to restrict whom you invite here on my account."

Mrs. Stapleton waved her hand. "It is no sacrifice on my part. I am delighted to have you and Miss Bennet as my guests, and I want to ensure you will both enjoy your time here."

I met Mrs. Stapleton's gaze. "I appreciate that."

"You are most welcome, my dear."

Aunt Gardiner drummed her fingers upon her thigh. "It was an odd coincidence for me to meet the Darcys tonight. As a child, I lived five miles from Pemberley, the Darcys' estate. The late Mr. Darcy and Lady Anne Darcy had sterling reputations, and they were a striking couple. People used to speak of them with reverence. My family moved from Derbyshire to London twenty years ago—Lady Anne Darcy still lived then. I believe she died shortly after Miss Darcy's birth." Her sight shifted to me. "At any rate, I caution you not to raise your hopes that Mr. Darcy intends to court you. I fancy he is a busy man, and we do not know when or if we shall see him or his sister again."

"Well, Miss Darcy invited me to tea tomorrow, but she did so without her brother's prior knowledge. It is possible he will not approve."

Mrs. Stapleton clapped her hands. "Oh, that is excellent! I should wager he will be more than pleased at his sister's initiative. Although your engagement is with Miss Darcy, I expect the gentleman will make an appearance whilst you are there."

My aunt beheld me, her expression severe. "I am responsible for your welfare while we are here, so I admonish you to never spend time alone with Mr. Darcy. After all, we cannot be certain of his nature on such a short acquaintance."

"I understand." Our host's whimsical imagination had led Aunt Gardiner to fret needlessly. After all, why should I ever be alone with Mr. Darcy? Nevertheless, the mere concept provoked a pleasant shiver. Without doubt, I welcomed the opportunity to meet him again. In fact, if I received a note from Miss Darcy cancelling our engagement, I should be dejected.

CHAPTER 2
A Bond of Friendship

Tuesday, 6 August
Ramsgate

"AHA!" I CROUCHED TO PICK UP A NARROW PIECE OF driftwood. "This will do quite well for you, my boy." In my haste to leave the house this morning, I had neglected to bring my collie's beloved ball. I raised the stick to a chorus of Rory's joyous barks. After a feint, I threw it. He sped off in pursuit, kicking up a spray of sand.

"Good morning, Miss Bennet." The melodious voice—*Mr. Darcy's*—sent my pulse soaring.

I pressed a hand to my heart and willed it to calm before spinning towards him. "Good morning, Mr. Darcy." He had played a significant role in my preposterous dream last night, in which we had met in London, formed a fast friendship, and gone on a madcap adventure together, although most of the specifics eluded me. In reality, his alluring aspect and commanding presence imparted a far greater effect upon me than in my dream: my legs quivered, and a feverish, almost rapturous energy fuelled me, urging me to move closer to him. But my sense of decorum prevailed, and I preserved a respectable distance.

Rory returned and dropped the stick between us, his tail wagging. Mr. Darcy took up the driftwood and threw it much farther than I could have managed. "If you would not mind my company, I should like to walk with you."

"You are welcome to join me." Within our first few steps together, Aunt Gardiner's warning echoed in my head. Nevertheless, I dismissed the concern. No one could declare us to be alone when several others occupied the beach; besides, I had Rory with me.

In the guise of viewing the incoming tide, I sneaked glimpses at him. Did I dare hope he had sought me out? A moment later, the likely reason for him doing so occurred to me: he may intend to rescind his sister's invitation. I could not bear to continue in suspense, so I cemented my sight to the sandy ground whilst I worked out how to proceed. "Last night at dinner, Miss Darcy suggested I have tea with her today, but I understand if it is not convenient."

"On the contrary, my sister is in great anticipation of seeing you."

I met his dark, magnetic eyes, but I soon had to wrest my sight from him lest I continued to stare. "I am...um...glad to hear it."

"I enjoyed our discussion of John Locke's works. I appreciate the way you entertained my ideas and expressed your own with confidence and clarity. It is rare, in my experience, for someone with strong opinions to handle challenges to their beliefs with ease and give fair consideration to opposing views."

"Yes, most people resist deliberating arguments that contradict their preconceived notions, and it is a shame—conversation would be dull without the occasional disagreement. But I suppose there is a certain comfort in believing your opinions are correct."

"No doubt that is true."

"In my case, I am accustomed to having my assertions challenged. My father has granted me free access to his library, and we often debate the concepts presented in the books we have both read."

"Did you attend a seminary?"

My step faltered. Would he be dismayed at my answer? "No, and neither did my sisters and I benefit from a governess or companion. Those of us who had the interest, read on our own. My father assisted me in grasping the more challenging components of mathematics, physics, and philosophy." I ventured a glance at him; he showed no sign of disapproval.

"Formal schooling has its drawbacks. My sister received most of her education at home. When Georgiana was fourteen, I followed my aunt Lady Matlock's recommendation and sent her to a renowned school for girls in London, but she hated the place—several of her school-fellows were cruel to her. I took her home well before the end of the term, and she never went back."

"I am sorry to hear that. Girls can be selfish and thoughtless at that age. Does Miss Darcy have a companion?"

His jaw clenched. "Not at present. I am in search of a new companion for her. The last one proved to be...unsatisfactory."

Oh dear, it seemed I touched upon a sensitive topic. With a slight shake of his head, he regained his former equanimity. Still, I sought a new subject. "My aunt and I are here for the month of August. How long will you and Miss Darcy remain in Ramsgate?"

"For a few more weeks at least." He bent his head to regard me. "Is this your first visit to Ramsgate?"

"Yes. I love it here—the invigorating sea breeze, the sounds of the waves and the gulls—it is all so soothing. Of course, I am fond of Hertfordshire, where I grew up, as well."

"I have passed through the area many times, and the countryside is beautiful. I am partial, though, to the rolling hills, moorlands, and limestone gorges that comprise Derbyshire."

"That is not surprising. Nothing can compare to one's home."

"Where in Hertfordshire do you reside?"

"Our estate, Longbourn, is a few miles from Meryton."

"*Meryton.*" His head snapped towards me. "My friend Charles Bingley wrote to tell me that he signed a lease for a property near there called Netherfield Park."

"What a coincidence! Netherfield Park borders Longbourn to the north. I am glad to hear it will be occupied soon, for it has been vacant far too long. Will your friend take possession at Michaelmas?"

"He expects to arrive there earlier—the middle of September. There are repairs to the house he intends to oversee."

My eyebrow arched. "I presume your friend will make us an amiable neighbour."

"Bingley is good-natured and garrulous. He is certain to be popular."

"That is welcome news."

"He has invited—"

A high-pitched yelp pierced my ears, and I whirled round. Rory limped towards me on three legs, his right front paw tucked under him. "Dear me, he must be injured." I rushed towards him, but Mr. Darcy reached Rory first.

He knelt before my dog and gently raised the favoured paw to reveal a protruding shiny object. "Miss Bennet, will you hold him to ensure he remains still?"

"Yes, of course." I crouched on the other side of Rory and curled my arm around his middle. I caressed his neck with my free hand. "Easy, boy."

Mr. Darcy cocked his head to scrutinise the wound. He handled the bit of metal in slow, careful movements. "Steady now, boy. I almost have it."

Rory released a soft whine.

"Forgive me, boy." He grimaced and removed the offending red-tinged object from Rory's paw. He held it out for my inspection. "A fish-hook."

"Thank goodness you got it out." I released Rory and stroked him behind the ears. "Poor boy, that must be painful."

"Luckily, the gash does not appear to be deep, but it should be attended to right away. I shall carry him back to the house." Mr. Darcy dropped the hook into his coat pocket.

"Oh...ah...very well." I moved to allow Mr. Darcy more space. He gathered Rory in his arms and stood. I walked at his side, giving my dog periodic pats. "Thank you, I appreciate your assistance."

"I am pleased to help."

My sight lingered upon the sleeve of Mr. Darcy's fine merino coat. As might be expected, the sea water and beach had rendered

Rory's fur damp and untidy. However, in addition to particles of sand and dog hair, a few scarlet droplets sullied the gentleman's garment. "I am sorry—your coat is stained with blood."

"It is of no consequence."

Based upon our first meeting, I should have assumed him to be fastidious with regard to his looks, but that must not be the case. At least, if it distressed him to soil his expensive clothing, he hid it well. Affection for him surged in my breast; his ability to elicit my esteem appeared to be boundless.

At the house, I directed Mr. Darcy to the servants' entrance. He placed Rory upon a table and showed Peggy the lesion.

I walked Mr. Darcy to the door. "Thank you again. I am glad you happened to be with me this morning. I should like to think I could have removed the fish-hook myself, but the sight of blood has made me queasy in the past."

"That is understandable. I am pleased to have been of service." He passed over the threshold and looked my way. "Until this afternoon, Miss Bennet."

"Until then, Mr. Darcy."

He sent me a smile before he departed, and I forgot to breathe. I remained there, staring at the closed door until my thudding heart resumed a regular beat.

I continued on to my room and collapsed upon the bed. Even though I had parted from Mr. Darcy mere minutes ago, the anticipation of seeing him again that afternoon dominated my thoughts. What had come over me? Never before had I been so drawn to another person. My youngest sister, Lydia, often became infatuated within moments of meeting a gentleman, but not me. I had too much sense to succumb so easily to a near-stranger, or so I should have averred yesterday.

Why did he hold such fascination for me? It went far beyond his physical allure, though everything from his noble visage to his euphonious voice and his peculiarities of manner enticed me. Maybe because, despite my lack of wealth, conventional education, or social standing, he appeared to value my opinion.

Last night, he had apologised for his initial rudeness and had gone out of his way to gain my dog's approval. This morning, he had ministered to Rory's injury without hesitation. Thus far, he had shown himself to be a masculine ideal in intellect and sympathy—the likes of which I never expected to meet. Still, I needed to keep in mind that it would take time to be certain of Mr. Darcy's character. I should remain wary for signs of an objectionable side to his nature.

Darcy House, Ramsgate

The butler swept his hand towards the hall. "Please follow me, Miss Bennet."

I parted from Peggy, who had accompanied me on the walk from Mrs. Stapleton's home, to follow the tall, elderly man. He led me to an elegant drawing-room replete with sumptuous, yet tasteful, furnishings.

"Miss Bennet." The butler bowed and departed.

A beaming Miss Darcy shot up from the sofa and rushed towards me. "I am so glad you came!"

"Of course I did." I tilted my head. "Did you think I should not?"

She sobered for a moment. "Well, I have learnt to be cautious at taking people at their word." She motioned to the area behind her. "Please, have a seat."

"Thank you." I settled on the sofa and glanced around the room. Mr. Darcy's absence preoccupied me, yet I resisted asking after him —I had come at *Miss* Darcy's invitation.

She sat beside me. "I am eager to become better acquainted with you. I do not often meet ladies near my age. Of course, I realise I am younger than you. I am fifteen, but my birthday is next month."

"And I am twenty."

"Oh, I had guessed you to be eighteen or nineteen, not that it matters to me." Her brow crimped. "I hope...um...*you* do not mind that I am younger than you."

"No, not at all. My best friend happens to be seven years older than I am, but I also have friends who are younger. And I have three younger sisters."

"I asked Fitzwilliam to join us at half past one. I wanted to spend time alone with you first. I thought...um...in private, it would be easier for us to have a candid conversation."

"I see." I took in Miss Darcy's shrunken posture. What could be weighing upon her?

"Fitzwilliam is a wonderful brother. I should not want you to think badly of him for the way he acted towards you when we first met."

"Please do not give that a second thought. I accepted his apology."

"Yes, but I want to explain why he mistook your motives. Although I am not out yet, my brother allows me to attend small gatherings with friends and neighbours. Since my arrival in Ramsgate, I have met several young ladies who stay in town. Two of them in particular shared a close bond, and they appeared to want to befriend me. For a while, I took delight in their company. Last week, my brother and I attended a garden party, and I walked by those two ladies whilst they talked with a third lady."

She averted her gaze. "I overheard them disparage me. They lamented having wasted so much time in my company since my brother had never been present during any of their calls."

"I am so sorry." I patted her hand. "Those two young ladies are despicable, and you are well rid of them."

"Thank you, I agree." She gave me a weak smile. "In any case, I told Fitzwilliam that I felt ill and needed to return home. Later, I related what had happened, and he became quite upset on my behalf."

Mr. Darcy's shocking accusation from Saturday morning echoed in my ears. Without doubt, his words had portrayed a protective—and presumptive—brother rather than a conceited prig, as I had first assumed. How wrong I had been! "I appreciate you sharing this with me."

She nodded.

"It occurs to me there is one advantage to lacking wealth or an esteemed family name—any friends I make are apt to be sincere since they cannot expect any material advantages from the association."

"Well, I should be pleased to call you a friend."

"The feeling is mutual. My friendship is yours if you want it."

"Yes, most definitely." Miss Darcy clenched her hands into a ball. "But you may grow weary of me. I fancy I must be naive and dull in comparison to your other friends."

"No, that is not the case. I enjoy your company. Although our acquaintance is new, I have learnt you are a kind person who shares my affinity for music and dogs, among other things." I grinned at her. "Rory likes you, so you must be a good person." My words failed to brighten her comportment.

"I want to believe you, but in all honesty, it is difficult for me to distinguish insincerity in others."

The poor girl—those two young ladies had damaged her self-esteem. "Despite your experience with those two pseudo friends, I believe most people are trustworthy."

"The truth is..."—her voice grew soft—"they were not the first to betray my trust."

"Oh dear."

"I came to Ramsgate with my companion. I liked her very much and believed she cared about me. But she conspired with a person I have known since childhood in a cruel plan to deceive me. To my good fortune, my brother arrived unexpectedly and intervened. He saved me from...um...well, he ensured their scheme did not succeed."

Oh no, she has endured so much! "That must have been a frightful ordeal. Thank goodness Mr. Darcy thwarted their design. What happened to the companion and her accomplice?"

"My former companion gave my brother a written confession and agreed to never again seek work in that field in exchange for his not taking her to the magistrate. And the other person is in debtors' prison." Her lips compressed. "I had been keen to leave

Ramsgate, but my brother convinced me to stay—he did not want my affection for the town to be destroyed by their treachery."

"I am glad you remained. I hope you are as well."

"Yes, I am."

"It is dreadful to have a close friend disappoint you. Although my experience differed from yours, it happened to me as well."

Miss Darcy's azure irises centred upon me. "That is unfortunate. If you do not mind telling me, I should like to know what happened."

"I do not mind. Five years ago, a young lady I had known since childhood inherited a large sum of money from a distant relative. Soon thereafter, she and her family moved to London. We agreed to correspond and visit each other as often as possible. But after she sent a few letters to me, she stopped writing. It disheartened me." I ground my teeth as memories from that time descended upon me. "I presumed she decided her old friends no longer had a place in her new life."

"Oh, that is sad. Did you ever hear from her again?"

"No. Last year, one of the London newspapers announced her marriage to a Mr. Mowbray. I sent her a letter of congratulations, but she never replied."

"Mowbray." Miss Darcy blinked at me. "The name sounds familiar—although I have never met him or his wife, I believe the gentleman is an acquaintance of my brother's."

"I ought to have been more discreet and omitted the name. I should have been mortified to learn Mrs. Mowbray was a friend of yours."

"Not at all. I am glad you took me into your confidence. And if you ever write to me, I promise to always send you a response."

"Thank you, that means a great deal to me. I should be happy to correspond with you after I return to Hertfordshire." I asked Miss Darcy to describe the concerts she had attended in Ramsgate, and that led to an animated conversation. A pair of maids entered with refreshments, and minutes later, brisk footsteps heralded Mr. Darcy's arrival.

I broke off mid-sentence, and my eyes flew to him. In that moment, all other thoughts dispersed.

"Good afternoon, Miss Bennet."

"Good afternoon, Mr. Darcy." It seemed the room had grown warmer, for perspiration glued the fabric of my dress to my back, and fire scorched my face.

He sat across from us, and Miss Darcy poured the tea. His gaze locked upon me. "How is Rory?"

Under his scrutiny, my mouth went dry, impelling me to swallow. "He is well, thank you."

For Miss Darcy's benefit, I explained what befell my dog that morning.

"Poor Rory." Miss Darcy's brows drew together. "I hope he heals swiftly."

"Thank you. I do as well, for he will be keen to resume his walks as soon as possible."

Mr. Darcy cleared his throat. "Until your dog recovers, you will be deprived of your companion for your morning jaunts. I do not presume to be Rory's equal, but I should be pleased to serve in his stead."

What a welcome suggestion! I edged forwards in my seat. "I accept your kind offer. I should be glad to have a substitute walking companion, even a mere two-legged one." He responded with an engaging grin. The hours until tomorrow morning could not pass fast enough to suit me.

In time, though, a touch of unease tempered my mirth. Aunt Gardiner would not approve of this arrangement. Well, I should not mention it to her.

Friday, 9 August
Ramsgate

I neared the beach and scoured the area for Mr. Darcy without luck. My steps floundered to a halt. Had he forgotten about me? I should not be surprised; a busy man like him must have many demands upon his time. But this reasoning failed to diminish my disappointment.

On the previous two mornings, he had awaited me on the stone slope near the entrance to the strand. Whilst I had treasured every moment of our time together, maybe he had been less affected. Could it be that he had viewed our walks as a mild amusement, a way to pass the time, and had tired of me? No, that could not be true; or did I fool myself?

Perhaps he had been delayed. I succumbed to my eagerness to see him and veered towards his residence.

I spotted him near the steps to his house speaking with a tall grey-haired gentleman. Based upon their tense postures, they must be having an animated discussion or perhaps even an argument. When I came within twenty yards of the pair, Mr. Darcy caught sight of me and waved. He exchanged a few more remarks with the flinty-eyed stranger, then parted from him and strode towards me.

"Forgive me for being late, Miss Bennet." He displayed a winsome smile. "I had been on my way to meet you when my friend called."

"Think nothing of it. I hope you did not cut your conversation short on my account." I glanced towards the tall man's retreating figure—he tramped away with his head lowered. "Your friend appeared to be discontented. I hope nothing is amiss."

"No, not at all." Mr. Darcy responded in a rushed cadence. "He had a business proposition for me, and I declined it." He held out his arm.

"Oh, I see." My hand curled around the proffered limb. I could not cast off the conviction that he had not been candid. I itched to press him further but restrained myself. After all, I had no right to pry into his personal affairs.

"Is Rory's paw healing well?"

"Yes, I think he may be recovered enough to walk out with me tomorrow."

"Ah, that is...good news." He tipped his head to view me with a tentative smile. "Of course, when that occurs, my justification for accompanying you ceases to exist. Will you allow me to escort you once Rory's presence makes me superfluous?"

"I should be pleased to have your company with or without Rory."

"That is good to hear."

Under the scope of his enthralling eyes, heat seared my cheeks. In truth, I should have been forlorn if he had ceased walking with me. Despite the delightful charm of Ramsgate and the gracious company of Mrs. Stapleton and my dear aunt Gardiner, my most cherished moments of this trip had been spent with him. He brought out a wealth of foreign feelings in me—an elated giddiness and an elusive yearning, as well as a fulfilment the likes of which I had never experienced. Time with him always raced by, leaving me in anticipation of our next meeting. A distant inner voice warned me to guard my heart, for this sweet interlude would end upon my departure from Ramsgate, but I had no will to heed the admonition.

Thursday, 29 August
Stapleton House

My eyes flew open. *Oh no—what time is it?* Glaring sunlight streamed in from the window, illuminating the room. I threw off the bedclothes. I had overslept, and of all the worst times to do so, with just two days remaining of my sojourn. Even if Miss Darcy and I exchanged letters in the future, once I left Ramsgate, I might never see *him* again.

I glanced at the bracket clock on the table. I had slept a full ninety minutes past my usual rising time. He would have waited a while for me but not for this long. No doubt he had returned home by now.

Nevertheless, I leaped off the bed and rushed through my ablutions. With Peggy's assistance, I dressed in a flash and left the house with Rory at my heels. I searched the area where he had met me on previous mornings to no avail. I continued along the beach in an aimless fashion. My shoulders sank and moisture pricked at my eyes, but I tried to reason myself out of my gloom. Although I should not see him today, since Mrs. Stapleton had planned an excursion to an adjacent town, I should walk with him tomorrow morning and apologise then. And Mrs. Stapleton had invited the Darcys to dinner tomorrow night.

Rory barked and trotted ahead up the beach towards the two Miss Smiths—elderly sisters who lived nearby. The spinster ladies, as a rule laconic and staid, demonstrated an unusual degree of esprit in their conversation with...*Mr. Darcy*. My legs propelled me in a fluid, vigorous pace.

His eyes fixed upon me, and a smile lit his countenance. After a few more words to the two ladies, he came to meet me. The Miss Smiths waved, and I returned the greeting.

"Good morning, Miss Bennet. Are you well?"

"Good morning, Mr. Darcy. Yes, I am. Please forgive me for keeping you waiting. I overslept. I do not understand, since this never happens to me."

"It seems it does." He crouched to give Rory a pat. "You must have needed the rest."

"In any case, I shall ensure it does not happen tomorrow. I am glad you found a source of amusement in my absence."

He stood. "If you refer to the Miss Smiths, I spoke with them for ten minutes at most, although...it seemed longer."

"From what I could tell, you had them thoroughly charmed. I dare say you made their morning walk memorable."

"If you are correct, I surpassed my goal of acquitting myself with a modicum of success. I often fumble for what to say in such circumstances." He held out his arm, and I took it. He led us to a path between the houses and the beach.

"Thank you for waiting. Had you returned home, I should not have blamed you." I refrained from adding that I should have been disappointed in that event.

"I should not have left. If you had taken much longer, I should have enquired after you at the house."

"Oh. At this hour?"

"I should have gone to the servants' entrance."

The intense blaze in his eyes made my mouth go dry, inhibiting my ability to speak—a fortunate occurrence, for otherwise I may have babbled on in an incoherent fashion. We continued to an area beyond the houses.

"Do you mind if we sit on the rocks along the cove?" Mr. Darcy pointed to a stone formation in an area secluded from the main path.

"No, not at all."

He led me inside the cove and bade me to sit upon a large, flat boulder. I left room for him, but rather than make use of it, he stood before me. "I keep reminding myself that we met less than a month ago. Yet my former existence—when you did not occupy my mind day and night—seems foreign to me. I am indelibly altered now, and I cannot contemplate a future that does not include you."

My breath rushed out, and my fingers gripped the hard surface of the rocky seat lest I tottered. His words surpassed my wildest hopes!

"Unless I have deluded myself, I believe you have developed tender feelings for me as well. Am I wrong?"

"No, you are not."

He held out his hand, and I extracted my fingers from the stone to link with his. Sparks shot through my hand—my entire arm. He knelt upon one knee. "Miss Bennet, my love for you is so wondrous and engrossing, it surpasses any sensation I have ever experienced. This adoration has turned my world on its head, and none but you could set it aright again. Will you do me the honour of accepting my hand in marriage?"

"I thank you for your offer." My voice quavered. "I am delighted to accept."

His resultant grin transformed him, crinkling his eyes whilst lending him a more youthful, blithe appearance. He lifted my hand to bestow a kiss. "Thank you...Elizabeth."

My upper body trembled through my next exhalation. Never had my name sounded so euphonic. This seemed too incredible to be real—that the man who had stolen my heart would be my husband.

He sat beside me, retaining my hand. "I had wondered if you might need time to decide. If so, I should have waited for as long as you needed." He raised an eyebrow. "Still, if we could wed tomorrow, I should prefer nothing more."

"My feelings are much as you described. A few weeks ago, I had no idea love could be so fulfilling and yet so consuming. I could not bear the thought of leaving here and never seeing you again, though I had assumed it would be the case. If I had my way, we should never have to part."

"With your agreement, I hope we shall marry as soon as possible. Our wedding could be in Hertfordshire or anywhere else you prefer."

"I should need my father's approval as I am not yet of age. He may be shocked when he hears the news, but I do not expect him to withhold his permission. As for my mother, she..." I stiffened, a knot forming in my gut. I had hinted at the lapses of propriety certain members of my family had made in the past, but he had not met them. What if a first-hand view of my mother or younger sisters repulsed him enough to make him regret our engagement?

"What is troubling you?" Lines filled his forehead.

"I have described my family to you, but until you meet them, you will not comprehend the brunt of their...peccadillos." My chin sank.

"You ought to know that my relations are not models of perfect behaviour. I do not expect yours to be either."

"I appreciate that. But my family includes more than our share of *characters*, and they often mortify me in public. I think...um...it is best if we keep our engagement a secret until you have met them. That way, if you were to decide..." I could not bring myself to complete the sentence.

He squeezed my hand. "If you suppose I may be driven off by an eccentric or rude relative, you are mistaken." His thumb caressed my palm. "When I meet your kin, I shall keep in mind that they love you and have contributed to making you the person you are today. For that, they have my eternal appreciation."

My chest threatened to burst with love for him. What had I ever done to deserve such understanding and compassion? His devotion almost defied all sense—without doubt, he could have chosen a wealthy, well-connected, and beautiful lady of the highest circles. As I dwelled upon that fact, a part of me cried out for further assurance. "Why me?" I whispered the question.

He inched closer. "What did you say?"

"From what Mrs. Stapleton and my aunt have said, you could have your choice of ladies prominent in London—well-educated women with wealth and high social rank." An image of Miss Comerford intruded upon my mind, and I blinked to dispel it. "And in contrast, my dowry is nominal, and my family are apt to be more of a detriment than an asset to your rank. Most will consider your choice of wife to be a poor one."

He took a slow breath. "In the past, I had a more restrictive notion of the sort of lady I should marry. My late parents expected me to choose someone from a wealthy, well-connected family. But my experiences in the last few years have altered my outlook. I have befriended people from the lower classes and witnessed a great deal of dissolute behaviour from members of the gentry. I came to realise that what matters most to me in a future spouse is her character, not wealth, connexions, or standing. And above all, I want to marry for love."

"But why do you love *me*—of all the ladies you have met?"

"It may not be possible to explain why I feel such a powerful sentiment for you, but I shall try. I am drawn to you for your unique qualities—your intelligence and self-confidence, your generosity to friends and strangers alike, your love of animals and nature, your thirst for knowledge, and your enthusiasm for debate. And if that is not enough, your outward appearance is not the least bit offensive."

I chuckled. "Why, thank you, gallant sir, neither is yours."

His irises darkened. "You are beautiful, Elizabeth, inside and out.

Your fine, expressive eyes drew my notice at my first sight of you, despite my suspicion for your intent at the time. Were I granted the power, I should not alter any part of you."

"I cannot say I agree, but I am gratified by your words."

His mouth flattened. "Pray, what would you change if you could?"

I shrugged. "My elder sister is a true beauty. She is ideal in every way. I have often wished I had blonde hair like hers."

"I adore your raven, curly locks."

"Thank you. But my mane fights all attempts to tame it. As a matter of fact..." I untied my bonnet to redirect a lock that had worked its way out of the simple arrangement Peggy had used that morning.

"May I be of assistance?"

My hand froze. "Ah...yes, if you wish." I removed the loose hairpin that hung at a precarious angle and handed it to him.

After taking off his glove, he gathered the errant tress and re-pinned it. "Your hair is softer and silkier than I had imagined. Disobedient it may be, but it is also glossy and stunning. Dark locks suit you."

"Thank you." *Mr. Darcy arranged my hair!* Had he done this sort of thing before—with Miss Comerford? I swallowed. "I should not have supposed you to be dexterous with hairpins."

He emitted a short laugh. "I have never used one before, but I have observed my sister's abigail on a few occasions."

"Oh." The pressure that had built in my chest abated, and happiness flowed unfettered from my core to my extremities.

He drifted closer, his face inches from mine. "Elizabeth, I want to kiss you." His voice sounded low and almost raspy.

It seemed I had lost the power of speech, so I stretched towards him. He rested his hands on my shoulders, and his lips met mine, instigating a shock of sensation that spread within me. I closed my eyes and savoured his distinctive aroma, enhanced by the scented water—a blend of lavender and citrus—applied by his valet. Then he took me in his arms, and I pressed against the firm plane of his chest. His touch, his seductive warmth, and his enchanting kiss combined to intoxicate me. Never had I been so discomposed, nor so desirous to remain in that state. I should have done anything he asked.

He had already bound me to him—utterly and irrevocably.

CHAPTER 3
The Rigours of Town

Stapleton House, Ramsgate

"You are engaged…to Mr. Darcy?" Aunt Gardiner inched towards me, her eyes wide.

"Yes." My smile receded. "I thought you would be pleased." I had sought a private word with my aunt, and we sat facing each other in Mrs. Stapleton's sitting room.

"Oh, my dear, I am. Without doubt, he is a wonderful match for you, and your mother will be thrilled. But as you are under my care, I feel bound to ensure you have thought through this decision."

"Yes, I have."

"My goodness, Rebecca had the right of it from the beginning. Mr. Darcy's interest in you has been apparent these past weeks." She directed her index finger at me. "You, on the other hand, never revealed a peculiar sentiment for him."

"I kept my feelings hidden." At least I did when in company. "Because I never believed he would offer for me."

"I see." Her tone softened. "I know you would not choose a husband for his wealth and status, but you met Mr. Darcy a mere three weeks ago, and marriage is a *lifetime* commitment. Are you certain you know him well enough to accept him?"

"Without doubt, I am sure. I love him."

The tension in her facial muscles remained. "It must be flattering for you to have attracted the attention of a wealthy gentleman like him. He is good-looking, and after his initial show of rudeness to you, his conduct has been exemplary. Still, it takes time to know a new acquaintance well. Although you have shared company with him here and at his residence, I wonder if those occasions have been sufficient to allow you to judge his character."

I bit my lip. For the sake of allaying my aunt's concern, I needed to be frank with her. "You make a valid point. The truth is, I...um... have been meeting him each morning on my walks. So, I have had ample opportunities for frank conversations with him in addition to the other times we have met the Darcys."

"Oh my, I ought to have guessed." Her hand raised to her chest. "Please tell me he has not taken advantage of you in any way."

"No, of course not. He has been a perfect gentleman." Heat rose from my neck. When I last stood before the looking glass, my swollen lips had receded to a semblance of their usual appearance. He had not pressed me for anything further than that remarkable kiss—or rather kisses.

"I am relieved to hear it." She rested her clasped hands in her lap.

"Mr. Darcy offered to take us to London in his coach on Saturday."

"Hmm, that will be convenient—if we ride with the Darcys we need not use Rebecca's carriage."

Thank goodness—travelling with the Darcys would make the journey far more enjoyable. Mrs. Stapleton intended to remain in Ramsgate another month. "The Darcys will proceed to Hertfordshire next week and stay at one of the nearby inns. A friend of Mr. Darcy's has leased Netherfield Park. Once his friend takes possession, they will reside there."

"Ah, your family will have new neighbours soon." Aunt Gardiner's fingers drummed upon the arm of her chair. "I must send an express to your father. I suggest you prepare a letter for him that I may include. I fancy he will be astonished at your news...and sad at the notion of losing his favourite debate partner."

"Yes, I shall do that."

"My dear, forgive me for my earlier reticence. You caught me off guard with your announcement, but I am truly happy for you." Aunt Gardiner came forward to kiss my cheek, then resumed her seat.

"Thank you, I am elated and thrilled. And also a bit nervous."

"Why are you nervous?"

"Well, one consideration is the rather daunting prospect of being introduced to Mr. Darcy's friends and relations."

She gave me a dismissive wave. "You have the intelligence, instincts, and poise to do well in any crowd. I have no concern for you."

"I appreciate that. Of course, I cannot control what others in my family may do or say in company with Mr. Darcy or his friends and family."

"Yes, I see what you mean." Her head edged sideways. "Since we shall see your parents when we take you home, I shall enlist Edward to speak to your father, and I shall have a long talk with your mother—we shall convey the importance of your acceptance in London society. To that end, Edward and I shall urge them to hire a companion for your younger sisters."

"Oh, that is a wonderful idea." How would Papa respond to this suggestion? He disliked making changes to the household and tended to leave such decisions to Mama. "What if my father does not agree?"

"In that event, I advise you against inviting your family to London. But I do not expect it will come to that—although your father may cavil at first, he will see reason."

I expelled a heavy breath. "Thank you, Aunt."

"You are welcome, my dear."

Monday, 30 September
Darcy House, London

I sat in the large armchair by the fireplace, tucked my legs beneath me, and reached for the goblet of wine on the adjacent table. My sight roamed around the mistress's suite, adorned in tasteful shades of green and gold, as I sipped from the cup cradled in my palm.

The weeks of our betrothment had sped by in a felicitous haze. Fitzwilliam and I resumed our morning walks in Hertfordshire, and though it ought to have been impossible, my love for him had grown stouter by the day. Despite his reserved nature, he charmed my friends and family—my mother most of all—and he overcame Papa's initial mistrust of him, earning my father's respect and approval.

Of course, a few of my family members embarrassed me at times, but I had reason to hope for improvement—at least in my sisters. Thanks to the combined efforts of my aunt and uncle Gardiner, Papa had hired a competent companion for Mary, Kitty, and Lydia. By the eve of our wedding, Georgiana had formed tentative friendships with them.

By all appearances, the handsome and charming Mr. Charles Bingley, Fitzwilliam's friend who leased Netherfield Park, had fallen for my dearest sister Jane at first sight. My sister accepted his attentions with pleasure and declared him to be the most affable gentleman of her acquaintance.

I had secured my future felicity that morning in the Longbourn church by becoming Mrs. Darcy, and I took no little delight in the new appellation.

Earlier today, Fitzwilliam, *my husband*, had led me through the rooms of his spacious, elegant house with unconcealed enthusiasm and a fair dose of pride—not that this stunning home did not merit the emotions. He had encouraged me to alter the furnishings as I desired, but I should be hard-pressed to find anything I disliked.

The day after tomorrow, we should leave for Brighton. Upon our return from the seaside, we should spend four months in London to effect my introduction to society.

My fingers traced the lace trim of my satin nightgown—a gift from my aunt Gardiner, who had assured me that Fitzwilliam would approve of the sleeveless garment.

At the knock upon the door to the master's suite, I set down the wine and stood, arranging my tresses, still damp from my bath, in front of me. "Come in."

Fitzwilliam entered the room and came to me. He wore a simple banyan of blue silk and had never looked more handsome. He stared at me, his face a reflection of awe or reverence. "You are exquisite—a vision of beauty." He fondled my hair, weaving his fingers through the strands, then set it behind my shoulders. His warm hands took hold of mine. "You are cold."

"No, or at least, not aside from my hands. And you are already remedying that."

"I love you so very much." Before I could form a reply, his mouth seized mine in a deep kiss. I stifled a groan, and that familiar drunken sensation impelled me to press against him lest I wobble. When he withdrew his lips, he left captivating kisses upon my face and the side of my neck where I am particularly ticklish, prompting me to flinch and giggle.

His eyes held me and darkened. With no apparent effort, he swept me into his arms. He walked to the bed, laid me down, and sat beside me. "Although the prevailing belief is that a wife is to submit to her husband, I do not want that for us."

I raised upon my elbows. "What do you mean?"

"I expect you to tell me if you do not want to be intimate with me—tonight or any time in the future. I shall never force you, for I want you to be a willing participant. And if you ever want me to stop, let me know."

"I appreciate that. Rest assured I am willing, and I want to please you."

"And I very much want to give you pleasure. Although it is likely our first joining may cause you pain, I shall do my best to minimise it."

"I understand, and I am ready."

He brushed his hand along the side of my nightgown. "As lovely as this is, I should prefer to remove it."

"Oh?" I gulped. "Is that...customary?" And could I do this—be completely naked before him?

"I know not, and I shall not do it unless you consent."

As much as I wanted—needed—to make him happy, how could I refuse? "No, or rather, yes. I want you to do whatever you wish. I trust you."

"Thank you, my love." He raised the skirt of my nightgown, and I moved my hips to allow him to take it higher, baring my lower body. He paused to leave a soft kiss upon my stomach before he slipped the garment over my head and tossed it onto a nearby chair. His brown eyes met mine. "Every part of you is beautiful."

With effort, I fought the inclination to curl up and cover myself. A perturbing thought came to me: Had he viewed Miss Comerford's body? If so, mine would look inferior to hers. A moment later, though, I chastised myself for giving the woman a jot of consideration. The past did not matter; Fitzwilliam loved me. And I was his wife—till death did us part.

He removed his banyan, and my sheepish glances at him drew my admiration and fascination. I managed not to ogle him, but *good heavens*—his muscled and flawless figure rivalled the best Greek statues! He moved atop me, and before the supreme intimacy of our position could absorb me, he kissed and sucked gently at my throat whilst his hands explored and caressed me. He progressed in this manner to include my most sensitive and secret areas, creating such delectable tingles upon my skin and beyond that I could focus upon nothing else.

In his most lustful moments, I found my husband to be more irresistible than ever. And not once did I consider halting his ministrations—not any of the times we expressed our love that night.

My stars, how did this ever come to be termed a *duty*?

Tuesday, 5 November
Stapleton House, London

My darling husband of five weeks leaned near my ear while we ascended the steps of the majestic stone home. "You are beautiful."

A delectable shiver coursed through me. How did he know I needed encouragement at that moment? Perhaps my mask of confidence had slipped. I gave him the smile he adored. He had complimented me earlier, though with different words, but I welcomed this well-timed advance of assurance. "Thank you, my love."

We had spent a blissful sojourn at a charming cottage in Brighton. Ten days ago, we returned to London, and Georgiana joined us from the Matlocks' home the following day. Based upon my correspondence with Jane, she and Mr. Bingley continued to grow closer. Perhaps her next letter would announce their engagement.

Last week, Fitzwilliam and I attended a party given by Lord and Lady Matlock, as well as several social gatherings at the homes of neighbours. The countess had specified which invitations ought to be accepted, and I met more people on those occasions than in my entire previous existence. Most of them proved to be, if not amiable, at least bearable. At tonight's soiree, I should become acquainted with still more.

Mrs. Stapleton gave us a warm greeting, and we sat together in the drawing-room. She poured cups of tea. "Thank you both for agreeing to come early tonight."

"It is our pleasure." I accepted a porcelain cup from her. "You are one of the few true friends I have in this town."

My husband glanced at me with a smile. "Indeed. I could never refuse the lady who is responsible for my current state of happiness."

Mrs. Stapleton raised a hand to her chest. "It is a delight to witness the pair of you. I had an inkling you two would have an affinity, and I could not be more delighted to have been correct." She eyed Fitzwilliam, tilting her head. "I detect a distinct alteration in you as a married man—an added vigour and contentment evident in your comportment."

"Without doubt, any improvement in me is due to my wife. She has influenced me for the better."

I sampled my tea. "As you can see, Mr. Darcy is the ideal husband—he suffers from a merry delusion in which my good qualities are exaggerated and my faults minimised."

Mrs. Stapleton's grin took on a smug cast. "With the astounding success of this introduction, perchance I shall try again with another bachelor. I have an unmarried lady in mind who might make a fine match for Lord Kentwood. It is high time he took a wife."

"No, I should not advise that." The vehemence in Fitzwilliam's response drew my notice.

"Whyever not?" Mrs. Stapleton's brows twitched. "I do not know Lord Kentwood well, but I have always observed him to be polite and charming."

"He would not be a...satisfactory husband for *any* decent lady."

"Upon my word, I am dismayed to hear it. Of course, appearances can indeed be deceiving. I am glad to know your opinion, and I shall bear that in mind for the future." She grimaced. "Oh dear, I have invited him here tonight—I hope that does not present a problem."

"Do not be concerned." Fitzwilliam offered her a pained smile. "At an occasion such as this, he will be on his best behaviour."

We spent a pleasant half an hour in conversation with Mrs. Stapleton in which she sought our impressions of Brighton and shared anecdotes of her previous stays in the seaside town.

A bustle of footsteps and voices in the hall heralded the arrival of several parties of guests at once. When the group entered the drawing-room, an odd phenomenon drew my attention: the newcomers gave a wide berth to an attractive, brown-haired gentleman of perhaps five-and-twenty.

Fitzwilliam led me straight to the man, who beheld us with an earnest, solemn expression. "Haddington, it is good to see you." My husband extended his hand.

Mr. Haddington gave Fitzwilliam's hand a hearty shake. "Darcy, I congratulate you on your marriage. I am happy for you."

Although he did not smile, the gentleman's speech bore the ring of sincerity.

"Thank you, I appreciate that." Fitzwilliam's sight veered to me. "Mrs. Darcy, I should like to introduce Mr. Cecil Haddington. He is an old friend."

"It is a pleasure to make your acquaintance, Mr. Haddington." I curtsied as the gentleman bowed.

"I assure you, the pleasure is all mine, Mrs. Darcy."

My husband's forehead furrowed. "I understand your uncle is... residing with you now. How is he?"

Mr. Haddington glanced at the floor. "Thank you for asking. He has fallen into a severe depressed state. Thus far, nothing I have said to him has had any effect."

"I am sorry to hear it. Do you think it might help if I called on him?"

"It is kind of you to offer, but I am afraid it would be a waste of time." Mr. Haddington frowned. "Yesterday, two of his closest friends came to the house, and he refused to see either of them."

"Well, if he becomes more amenable to company, let me know."

"Thank you, I shall."

After we parted from Mr. Haddington, I selected a moment with no one nearby to indulge my curiosity. "Why do so many of the other guests avoid Mr. Haddington?"

Fitzwilliam inched closer. "Almost eighteen months ago, Haddington's father, the late Lord Carswell, was arrested and imprisoned on charges of treason. It seemed certain he would have been found guilty, but before his trial, he hung himself in his cell."

"Oh no, that is terrible!"

He nodded. "The scandal has been onerous for young Haddington, who was stripped of his title. I did what I could to support him, and I have urged others to do so as well. But as you saw, many of his former friends refuse to acknowledge him."

"It is a shame and quite unfair to Mr. Haddington." A recent memory came to mind. "Last week at Gunter's, a lady at a table near us disparaged him without bothering to moderate her voice."

Fitzwilliam sighed. "Yes, I heard the woman."

"People can be unpardonably cruel." I shook my head at a servant offering glasses of wine, and he moved on. "You asked after Mr. Haddington's uncle. Is he ill?"

My husband's chest heaved. "No. The former Colonel Ernest Haddington had unwittingly supplied the information his brother Lord Carswell sold to the French. The former colonel, whilst inebriated, revealed sensitive military plans to his brother on several occasions. Ernest Haddington had been ignorant of Lord Carswell's crimes and never benefited from them. Nevertheless, for his gross negligence, he lost his commission and spent almost a year in gaol. He completed his sentence a few days ago and resides with Cecil Haddington at the family home in town."

"Oh, I see." The sins of the late Lord Carswell weighed heavily upon the man's son and brother.

A well-dressed couple strode towards us. As they neared and the lady's face became distinct, my frame tensed.

The gentleman grinned at my husband. "Darcy, I have been eager to congratulate you on your marriage."

"Thank you, Mowbray." Fitzwilliam's sight flitted to me, and he introduced the man and his wife. I took in the familiar features of the friend I had once treasured; they now belonged to a stranger.

"Oh, but Lizzy and I are already well acquainted." Mrs. Mowbray beamed at Fitzwilliam and me in turn. "You may not know that I grew up in Hertfordshire, and your wife and I have been dear friends since childhood." Enthusiasm infused her speech.

"Indeed?" Fitzwilliam turned to me.

"Yes, Mrs. Mowbray grew up in Meryton, and we first met as children." I presented a wooden smile to my former friend.

My husband took a quick look towards a crowd of people across the room. "Ah, I am afraid you must excuse us. A friend of mine beckons."

"Oh yes, of course." Mrs. Mowbray leaned closer to me. "I am in anticipation of spending more time with you now that you are in town."

With a slight nod, I allowed Fitzwilliam to lead me away.

"Unless I am mistaken, you were less than pleased to reunite with Mrs. Mowbray."

"You are correct. I once considered her to be my closest friend. That changed when she inherited a windfall, moved to town, and dropped the acquaintance."

"I am sorry, my love."

"It is of no matter. I shall see her no more than is necessary."

My husband directed his sight over my right shoulder. "*Damn.*" He muttered the expletive.

"What is it?"

"Forgive me. Lord Kentwood is walking this way."

I sneaked a sidelong glimpse of the tall, striking, dark-haired gentleman striding towards us.

Lord Kentwood stopped before my husband. "Darcy, it has been a long while. My congratulations to you on your recent marriage."

"Thank you, Kentwood."

A pair of dimples emerged with Lord Kentwood's dashing grin as his gaze centred upon me.

My husband's jaw clenched. "Mrs. Darcy, I should like you to meet the Marquess of Kentwood."

I curtsied. "It is a pleasure to meet you, my lord."

The marquess performed a courtly bow. "I assure you, Mrs. Darcy, the pleasure is all mine. I understand you are from Hertfordshire."

"Yes. My father's estate is near Meryton."

His hazel eyes gleamed. "Ah, that is a mere twenty miles from here. Why have I never met you before?"

"Well..." In my peripheral vision, I caught my husband staring at the marquess with a haughty expression. I touched his arm. With a glance at me, Fitzwilliam's glare receded. "In the past, I rarely visited London." *And no doubt we moved in quite different circles.*

"I am delighted you are here now." Lord Kentwood remained another few minutes to laud a recent concert he had attended before he waved to a gentleman across the room and took leave of us.

With an audible release of breath, Fitzwilliam adopted a more relaxed bearing.

His animosity towards Lord Kentwood and warning to Mrs. Stapleton seemed incongruous with my first impression of the marquess. In the past, I had encountered several men whose lascivious stares, whether overt or surreptitious, made me cringe. In contrast, Lord Kentwood had been gallant and personable. I tugged on Fitzwilliam's sleeve. "He acquitted himself well. Is he really that bad?"

His irises blazed, and the colour in his complexion heightened. "The marquess is the worst sort of rogue. He is glib, charming, and presents an appearance of virtue, but it is a pretence. He is a dishonourable rake." His fingers threaded through mine. "Promise me you will avoid him."

I clutched his hand. "Yes, I promise."

Wednesday, 6 November
Darcy House

My eyes fluttered open. In the tree outside the bedroom window, a pair of sparrows chirped a cheerful choral. A modicum of morning light penetrated the bed curtains—I ought to get up now.

For me to do so, though, necessitated a delicate manoeuvre. Fitzwilliam lay behind and against me with his arm around my waist. His respiration had the slow, steady rhythm of deep sleep. *He* could afford the luxury of remaining here a bit longer, but I needed to rise now to allow time for a walk in Hyde Park that morning—a self-indulgence I had no intention of forgoing. In actuality, it could be considered a necessity since the exercise would provide me the fortitude to endure the day ahead.

I made a gentle, slow withdrawal from beneath my husband's

arm, but at his unintelligible mumble, I paused. Despite my best intentions, I had disturbed his sleep. I began again with even slower movements. Once I had removed the bed-clothes and sat up, his hand closed around mine.

"Stay."

My lips curved up. He was even more laconic than usual when he first awoke. "Good morning, my love. If you recall, I intend to take a long walk in Hyde Park this morning. After all, I must be at my best later to face society's mightiest dragons."

Beginning today, our knocker remained up to indicate we should accept callers. My object: receive a multitude of visitors whilst maintaining my poise and refraining from any impertinent, insulting, or otherwise inappropriate utterances.

Lady Matlock had asserted she would be here to support me today—a development I took with equal parts chagrin and gratitude.

With a heavy exhalation, he released my hand and ran his fingers through his dishevelled mass of wavy, black hair. "Yes, I remember, but you have no cause for concern. Every last one of them shall fall at your feet and declare me fortunate for having won your hand."

My smile took a wry twist. "Ha! I wish I could believe that. Your aunt's public support might sway the majority of them in my favour, but a few will be determined to hate me no matter what I say or do, either for my humble origins or for having taken a prized bachelor off the market." I pushed open the bed curtains and stood. "You need not accompany me if you are not so inclined. Perhaps you would rather ride." Thanks to Fitzwilliam's patient instruction, I had developed a modicum of skill on horseback. Today, though, I craved the physical activity of walking.

"I shall come with you." He raised a hand to cover a yawn and moved to the edge of the bed.

His simple assertion inspired a lightness in my limbs. I loved him so much! Despite the responsibility upon his shoulders, Fitzwilliam, thus far at least, dedicated as much of his time to me as possible. I had never expected this from him. In accordance with my observation of married couples throughout my life, I had suspected our future married existence would necessitate us being apart more often than together. Not even my uncle Gardiner, who spent long hours away from home five or six days each week, demonstrated as much devotion to my aunt Gardiner as Fitzwilliam did to me.

Hyde Park

Fitzwilliam and I strode arm in arm along the Serpentine River with Rory romping ahead of us. Rose bushes with a scattering of coral blooms bordered one side of the picturesque path. We maintained my preferred gait, a rapid pace that stretched my shortish legs to their limits, and I took deep inhalations of the faint floral scent in the air. The serene beauty of the park energised me and lifted my mood, as did my husband's assured presence.

He angled his head for a better view of me. "Are you anxious for what awaits you today? I should not have you fret over this."

"No, I shall thwart every attempt by your friends and neighbours to intimidate me." I used a blithe tone.

"And I hope you do not think Lady Matlock does not trust you to handle the visitors yourself today. I am certain she merely wants to ensure your first day of calls is a pleasant one."

I nodded and turned away in case my countenance revealed my thoughts. Lady Matlock, although she and Lord Matlock had gone so far as to attend our wedding in Hertfordshire, had found a moment alone with me to relate her true opinion: she believed me to be unworthy of her nephew and considered our engagement to be the most foolhardy and regrettable act he had ever committed. Nevertheless, when Lord Matlock's most fervent arguments had failed to coerce Fitzwilliam to reconsider the decision, she had accepted the futility of any choice other than acceptance and resolved to make the best of the unfortunate situation. Ergo, she would do everything possible to encourage the most influential of her friends and acquaintances to accept me in order to minimise the injury to her nephew and niece.

For my part, I had swallowed my indignation and made no retort. I could not dispel the fear that she might be correct. Would our marriage damage Fitzwilliam's standing? Even worse, would it impair Georgiana's prospects since she had yet to make her debut? Either circumstance would be unendurable, so I resolved to gracefully accept Lady Matlock's assistance.

To her credit, the countess had displayed neither the poor manners nor the obtuseness of Lady Catherine de Bourgh, who had called on me in Hertfordshire one week before the wedding to hurl insults and demand I break my engagement. It seemed Lady Catherine had formed the mistaken notion that Fitzwilliam might marry her infirm daughter, Miss Anne de Bourgh.

In any case, I should not spoil my husband's idealised view of

Lady Matlock's motives; Lady Catherine's affronts had led to a heated argument between Fitzwilliam and she, and they had not spoken since. I refused to alienate him from another of his relations. By and by, I collected myself enough to provide him a verbal response. "I appreciate your aunt's assistance. I am not easily daunted, but this town can be confounding. It is akin to being in a foreign land where I do not always know who is a friend and who is a foe."

The skin around his soulful brown eyes creased. "You may be certain no one would dare treat you with disrespect in the presence of my aunt or me." At times like this, his overt concern for my comfort, in concert with his unrivalled handsomeness, took my breath away.

"Alas, I cannot use you and your aunt as shields all the time. You have perfected a menacing scowl that you employ to great effect. Maybe I should develop my own frightful glare." I drew to a tall, rigid position and demonstrated a fierce frown, one I used to direct at my younger sisters when they misbehaved. "How is this?"

A rumbling chuckle shook his chest. Once a rarity, the sound of his laughter, though no longer a novelty, remained precious to me. "That will never have the result you seek. You are far too beautiful and diminutive to scare anyone."

By now accustomed to his compliments, I refrained from protesting such extravagant statements. I exhaled in a huff for a feigned show of disappointment. "In that case, I must resort to being my charming self. If they do not like me, I shall not care a whit."

"Quite right."

My husband's encouragement combined with the exercise to deliver the desired effect upon me. With renewed confidence, I posed a related question that had niggled at me. "As you may recall, Lady Matlock intends to direct me in responding to the invitations we have received."

"Yes."

"In a couple of weeks, your aunt is hosting a ball in our honour, and we shall also be expected to host our share of dinner parties this Season as well. Knowing how, in general, you dislike such events, I wonder whether you are prepared for what is to come."

"Well, I should much prefer to take you and Georgiana to Pemberley now rather than wait for the spring..."

Lady Matlock had tried to convince Fitzwilliam that we should remain in town until the summer, but he refused to wait that long to show me his beloved estate.

"...but you need not be concerned for my sake. With you at my side, I have far more tolerance for these gatherings than ever before. Besides, I do not expect it to be so onerous. I imagine my aunt will press us to attend a couple of parties each week. In between, we shall see the Gardiners and attend concerts and plays. All considered, it will be bearable."

I grinned at his show of optimism. "I dare say we shall enjoy our stay in town." Armed with an idea of Fitzwilliam's expectations, I should stand firm against his aunt if she pressed me to commit to more than two events per week.

Darcy House

Fitzwilliam, Georgiana, and I discussed plans for the week while we awaited Lady Matlock's arrival in the green morning room. This warm, spacious area, featuring Egyptian-style rugs and window coverings, had been a favourite of Lady Anne Darcy's.

I had chosen to keep the original furniture here and have the faded fabrics replaced in a solid gold tint. I adored using the mahogany Chippendale writing desk that had once belonged to Fitzwilliam's maternal grandmother.

Slade, our staid and steady butler, appeared in the doorway. "Lady Matlock."

Egad, here we go. With a calming breath, I stood and rolled my shoulders back, locking them in place. I could not allow myself to slip into a lazy pose of the sort I once indulged in at Longbourn. The increased scrutiny that accompanied my new life as wife of an illus-trious gentleman required greater diligence from me, and today in particular I could not afford to look inelegant; I should make the best impression upon my dear husband's peers as possible.

My husband's striking aunt, whom I guessed to be near fifty years of age, exhibited a formidable presence despite her petite form. She strode into the room with an air of purpose.

I went to her. "Lady Matlock, thank you for coming."

She nodded, inspecting my attire. "You, or perhaps your abigail, chose well. You are neither underdressed nor betraying an obvious desire to impress."

"I am glad you approve." I moved aside so my husband and sister could greet their aunt. Fitzwilliam found my hand and squeezed it as he moved past me—a well-timed reminder of why I should treat Lady Matlock with more cordiality than my inclination.

Georgiana excused herself to practise her music, and her departure marked the disappearance of Lady Matlock's sanguine expression. The countess glanced around the room. "Yes, this area will serve well for your guests."

Her ladyship stepped towards me. "This is not quite right." Lady Matlock removed my silk scarf and tied it anew. Next, she peered at the careful arrangement of my hair; my abigail, Gibbs, had taken pains to make it appear stylish today. "Nor is this. Hold still for me." She loosened the primary knot and redid it, creating a less elaborate one. "Ah, that is better."

Had I looked too dressy for the morning? I raised an eyebrow at Fitzwilliam, and he shrugged.

Lady Matlock stepped back and placed her palms together. "Now, I should like to see the calling cards you have received."

"They are here." Fitzwilliam stepped to the desk, grabbed the salver that held the aforementioned cards, and handed them to his aunt. "I shall take my leave of you now. If you need me"—his eyes drifted to meet mine—"I shall be in my study." He kissed my hand and gave me a parting smile. When he left, a chill permeated the room.

After skimming through the cards, Lady Matlock pulled two of them out. "You must go through these on a daily basis and leave the most prominent names on top." She turned the two cards towards me so I could read the names: Lady Gillingham and Mrs. Drake. "These are the best of the lot. Keep in mind that many of the ladies visiting today will be eager to find any reason, no matter how small, to denigrate you to anyone who will listen."

"I understand." Would she ever cease speaking to me as though I had been raised by savages? Well, in her mind, maybe I had been.

"None of the ladies came in person, but it is no wonder since you sent your own calling cards out with a servant." Lady Matlock narrowed her eyes. "May I see your cards?"

"Of course." I had sent out two dozen of them the previous day pursuant to a list she had provided. I retrieved a silver case, a gift from my aunt Gardiner, from the desk and pulled out one of my cards.

Lady Matlock gave it a long stare before handing it back. "Yes, it is adequate. The script is simple and not too large." At the faint sound of a knock upon the front door, two creases appeared between her brows. "It is early for a call. Nevertheless, *you* must be all that is proper. Use this opportunity to demonstrate the gracious dexterity that must become second nature to you. A lady is *always* calm and serene. Never display strong emotions of any kind in the company of a guest. Can you manage this?"

Could I? A ball of panic took shape in my stomach, but I straightened my deportment and willed it away. "Yes, of course."

Slade appeared. "Mrs. and Miss Townshend have called, madam."

"Thank you, Slade. We are ready to receive them here." My voice sounded distant and formal as befitting the ideal, impassive society wife.

"Ah, this is a special case." Lady Matlock transitioned to an easy attitude. "With close friends, exceptions to the usual calling hours are acceptable. I trust you remember Mr. and Mrs. Townshend and their daughter Miss Barbara Townshend. You met them at the party last week."

"Yes, I do." The countess had mentioned the Townshends' long association with the Fitzwilliams and the Darcys, indicating they would be my allies.

Slade returned. "The Townshends."

How odd and unlike our fastidious butler—he neglected to name Mrs. Townshend and her two daughters. The younger of the pair, whom I had met, had dark blonde hair and blue eyes; I judged her to be near my age. The elder sister had not attended the party. She had golden blonde hair, twinkling chocolate eyes, and a bright, mischievous smile.

No sooner had I greeted Mrs. Townshend when Lady Matlock's overt gasp impelled me to spin towards the countess.

"My dear Mrs. Fraser"—Lady Matlock displayed a rare grin —"when did you return to England?"

The elder daughter, who must be Mrs. Fraser, strode forth and took the countess's hand. "But a few days ago, Lady Matlock. I surprised my family by arriving sooner than I had expected. My late husband's estate has been settled, so I shall remain in England for the foreseeable future."

The countess pulled the lady into an embrace. "I am delighted to see you again. I can fancy how happy your family must be to have you back home."

With a fond look at her eldest daughter, Mrs. Townshend nodded. "It is a great blessing to have Hannah and our granddaughter with us. We asked Slade not to announce her so you would be surprised."

Mrs. Fraser withdrew from Lady Matlock and turned towards me—an action that jolted the countess from her distraction enough for her to introduce us. Mrs. Fraser curtsied. "It is a pleasure to meet you, Mrs. Darcy."

"I am no less pleased to make your acquaintance, Mrs. Fraser." My sight flitted towards the other two Townshend ladies. "I am pleased to welcome you all to my home." We took seats, and I served the tea. Mrs. Townshend invited me, my husband, and my sister to dine at their residence the following evening, and I accepted.

While Miss Townshend spoke little, Mrs. Fraser revealed a depth of curiosity towards me, posing her questions with warmth and friendliness. Before long, she had coaxed me into a recital of how Fitzwilliam and I had met and our time spent in Ramsgate.

In turn, I learnt the former Miss Townshend had married a Scottish gentleman in 1808. Her husband had succumbed a year ago to bronchitis, leaving her with a young daughter, Violet. I expressed my condolences for her loss.

"Thank you." Mrs. Fraser leaned closer to me, tilting her head. "Um...Mrs. Darcy, I should not want to overstep, but do you suppose Georgiana and Mr. Darcy might be free? I should love to see them."

"That is a fine idea, Hannah." Mrs. Townshend shifted towards me. "It has been far too long since my daughter has laid eyes upon her dear friends."

Dear friends? An acrid taste filled my mouth. Fitzwilliam had never mentioned his 'friendship' with the former Miss Hannah Townshend. A pointed look from Lady Matlock made me start, and I set down my cup of tea. "Yes, of course. They ought to be able to join us." I rang for Slade and related my instructions.

Georgiana soon appeared. She ran towards Mrs. Fraser, giving her the second hug of her visit. "Mrs. Fraser, it has been so long. You look wonderful!"

When they separated, Mrs. Fraser peered at Georgiana. "You, my dear, have grown into a beautiful young lady. And you are so tall!"

"Yes, I believe I grew two inches in the past year. Will you stay in England?"

Sparks danced in Mrs. Fraser's irises. "Yes. It is wonderful to be home again."

My husband strode into the room and made an abrupt halt upon noticing Mrs. Fraser. His eyes widened before his expression transformed into a reflection of joy. "Hannah, you are here."

An icy bolt darted along my spine—he used her *given name.* What sort of association had this been?

Mrs. Fraser's demeanour, which had been open and easy a moment ago with Georgiana, remained complaisant, but her aspect hardened into a depiction of careful control. "Yes, Mr. Darcy, I am back in England for the foreseeable future."

My husband glanced my way, revealing a deeper colour than usual to his cheeks. But he regained his composure and gave warm greetings to Mrs. Townshend and Miss Townshend. When he stopped before the blonde widow, the pair commanded my full attention. "Mrs. Fraser, I am pleased you have returned."

The golden-haired lady replaced her strained smile with a more relaxed one and held out her hand. "It has been too long."

He shook her hand. "I trust Miss Fraser is well."

"Yes, she grows bigger each week, and her vocabulary expands by the day." She gave me a quick look. "I am happy to congratulate you on your marriage. Although I have just met Mrs. Darcy, I like her already. I hope we shall be good friends."

For what did I hope? At the moment, I wavered between longing for a true and dependable friend in the aloof world of London society and the desire for Mrs. Fraser to depart on a fast-moving coach back to Scotland—or anywhere but here.

"You and my wife share several common interests. I have no doubt the two of you will find amity."

Soon thereafter, Georgiana returned to the music room. Fitzwilliam too withdrew, mentioning correspondence he needed to address.

Once the Townshends had taken their leave, we returned to our seats in the green morning room. Lady Matlock sat back and crossed her ankles. "What a pleasant surprise to have Mrs. Fraser back in town. I encourage you to seek a friendship with her, for it will serve you well. She and her family are influential. They will persuade their friends to think well of you."

"I should be pleased to know her better." Although a plethora of questions concerning Mrs. Fraser consumed me, I should not expose my unease by querying my husband's aunt.

Slade returned and informed us of Lady Gillingham's arrival. The countess wrinkled her nose and stood. "Now it begins in earnest, for your next guest has a tendency to be thorny. Are you ready?"

"I am." I rose in preparation of greeting the formidable and crusty lady who bore no relevance to the perspiration on my palms.

CHAPTER 4
A Change of Plans

Darcy House

My sister viewed my husband whilst she carved a slice of beef on her dinner plate. "Fitzwilliam, was it not a delightful surprise to see Mrs. Fraser today?"

I almost winced at the name, which comprised a marked dissonance for me. My sight shifted to Fitzwilliam, seated across the dinner table, in anticipation of his response. His impassive expression did not alter.

"Yes, I did not expect to see her back so soon. In my most recent letter from Adam Townshend, he thought she would remain in Scotland until the end of April."

I took a sip of wine, determined to keep my disquiet at bay. "So, the Townshends have a son?"

Fitzwilliam met my gaze. "Yes, he attends Oxford."

"What is he like?"

"Young Townshend is amiable. I think he must be near one-and-twenty."

"And?"

"He is a bit shorter than me with a slighter build. He is blond-haired, like his sisters. I suppose most people would deem his appearance pleasing." His brow constricted, then relaxed. "Ah, you wonder whether he might be a match for one of your sisters."

"I believe you mean *our* sisters."

"Yes, of course."

"No, that prospect never crossed my mind. Georgie is not out, our younger sisters are not ready for marriage, and I hope Jane will be engaged soon. I simply wanted an idea of what to expect when I meet him, as I assume I shall in the future."

"No doubt you will. And I believe your elder sister will soon have felicitous news to share." His lips edged up.

"Oh? Has Mr. Bingley written to you?"

He nodded. "If all goes well, you will receive tidings of their engagement within the next fortnight."

"That is wonderful!"

"Yes, it is." A glimmer lit my sister's eyes. "I think Mr. Bingley is ideal for Miss Bennet."

"Thank you, Georgie." I beamed at her. "I could not agree more."

"I should be delighted to return to Hertfordshire for their wedding. I had such fun playing parlour games with Miss Kitty and Miss Lydia. And I purchased music for a sonata last week that I think Miss Mary would love to play. Maybe she would like to borrow it."

"I am certain she would."

My husband sent me a crooked smile conveying a silent tease, which I interpreted as: *Your influence has made my sister bolder than ever before.*

I responded with a self-satisfied grin, tipping an imaginary hat to him.

When Fitzwilliam enquired after my callers, I responded in my usual cheerful mode, disregarding the image of Mrs. Fraser that intruded upon my thoughts. I related a few of the encounters that day, leaving my most successful one for last—my time with Lady Gillingham. Upon our introduction at last week's ball, the woman had displayed cold disapproval for me. Lady Matlock had provided the probable explanation for her hostility: Lady Gillingham and Lady Catherine de Bourgh had been close friends since childhood.

I paused to consume a forkful of mashed potatoes. "Although Lady Gillingham greeted me with a haughty frown, within ten minutes we had progressed to making polite conversation. She asked me to join her for tea tomorrow and even expressed admiration for my gown."

"I am glad to hear it, and I am not the least bit surprised." My husband regarded me with a look of admiration. "No doubt, she could not help but like you despite whatever nonsense she may have heard from Lady Catherine."

"Although I should like to take credit for Lady Gillingham's change of heart, I cannot." I slipped a morsel of carrot into my mouth.

Fitzwilliam eyed me and set aside his fork, biding his time in anticipation of my conclusion.

Georgiana, though, lacked his patience. She leaned towards me. "I do not understand. What else could explain Lady Gillingham's altered behaviour with you?"

"Well, she brought Priscilla with her. And despite her declaration that her cat disdained all strangers at first, the creature took an instant liking to me." The angora cat, a gorgeous white specimen, had become an object of loathing to many of Lady Gillingham's friends and acquaintances. Nevertheless, they tolerated the finical feline in order to preserve the coveted connexion to the lady. "To my good fortune, Lady Gillingham appears to give greater weight to Priscilla's opinion than to Lady Catherine's."

Georgiana giggled. "From what I have heard, Lady Gillingham, like Priscilla, is difficult to please, so winning the approval of both of them is an impressive achievement."

"Indeed, it is a noteworthy triumph." Fitzwilliam raised his glass of wine to me. "Lady Gillingham's cat has a menacing sneer and is notorious for hissing and scratching at anyone who goes near it."

I had not yet witnessed my husband in company with the feline. "Have you ever been scratched by Priscilla?"

"No, but neither have I gone within three feet of the animal."

"Well, I shall do my best to convince Priscilla that you are tolerable."

His head slanted forwards. "Thank you."

~

Whilst I awaited my husband in our shared sitting room, I attempted to focus upon the novel that I had been reading, but after reviewing the same paragraph several times without comprehension, I snapped the book shut and set it upon my table. *Darn it*—I could not banish my jealousy of Mrs. Fraser. I had always associated that unbecoming sentiment with excitable, irrational, and weak-minded individuals. How had I allowed myself to fall victim to it?

Until I met Fitzwilliam, I had escaped its treacherous tentacles. I grew up alongside my eldest sister, whose beauty surpassed all others in the neighbourhood, without envying her. Moreover, I had no rational reason to justify my unease; my husband's love for me was overt and powerful, almost like a living, breathing entity—I did not question its existence.

Yet...what did I know of his *capacity* for love and affection? Could it be that men and women experienced these tender feelings in disparate ways? While my love for Fitzwilliam left no room for the possibility of caring for another man the same way, maybe his heart operated on a different scope. Goose-flesh erupted on my bare upper arms.

I stilled at the sounds of voices in the adjoining chamber: Fitzwilliam dismissed his valet, Winston. A moment later, my husband entered the room in his black velvet robe. I stood, and my earlier resolve to query him regarding Mrs. Fraser weakened. What if he affirmed my worst fears?

"My love, are you well?" Crinkles darkened his forehead as he covered the ground between us to take my hands. "You appear pale, and your hands are frigid."

I dredged up a smile, aiming to sound tranquil. "Yes, I am well. And you know my hands are often cold."

"Yes, but not this icy." He led me to the sofa, where we sat together, and I leaned against him. His arm curled around my shoulders, and his warm palm and fingers ministered to my hands, one at a time. In his presence, my earlier apprehension abated.

How should I word the questions that gnawed at my composure? I swayed to the side, meeting his dark eyes. "Why have you never mentioned Mrs. Fraser before?" He betrayed neither surprise nor alarm for the topic; so far, so good.

"Did I not?"

"I am certain you never did."

"My family and the Townshends have maintained a friendship since my childhood. We often saw them at dinners and parties. They have stayed at Pemberley several times, and they have hosted Georgiana and me at their estate in northern England. But in the past few years, I have only seen them in London."

I drew in a deep breath. "You called Mrs. Fraser by her given name today."

"Yes, I know. It must have been due to my surprise at seeing her. I have always called her Miss Townshend or Mrs. Fraser."

I edged away from him, and his arm fell to his side. "It is a very odd error for you, of all people, to have made."

"Why do you say that?"

"I can picture almost anyone else making a similar blunder, but not you. Your friends and family postulate your precise nature, and I have never observed you to be so flustered in company before."

"Nevertheless, it has happened. I make mistakes like anyone else. I have often heard her family members refer to her as 'Hannah', so it is an understandable error."

"Did you ever consider Mrs. Fraser as a potential spouse?"

"No, we were always friends, nothing more."

I studied him and kneaded my upper arms since the goose-flesh had returned. He displayed every appearance of sincerity, but would he dissemble to conceal a truth that would pain me? "I should wager your family deemed her to be the perfect lady for you."

His hand landed on my shoulder and stroked my tense muscles. "*You* are my ideal match. I have met plenty of ladies who might have made me a *satisfactory* wife, but none of them compared to you."

A welcome warmth spread through my core, and the pressure in my chest diminished. I had never needed his reassurance more than at that moment. I did not doubt him, but a sudden intuition directed my next question. "If you never courted Mrs. Fraser, then you must have been happy for her when she became engaged."

His mouth flattened. "As a matter of fact, no. I was...concerned for her. She had only known Mr. Fraser for a few weeks when she accepted his proposal. Furthermore, he had insisted on a three-week engagement, citing the need to return home to Scotland."

"*We* had known each other no longer than that when you proposed to me, and our engagement ran a similar course."

He released a short laugh. "Until I met you, I should have considered three weeks to be an inadequate amount of time to judge another person's character. Now I know better."

"Did you have a reason to disapprove of Mr. Fraser?"

"I had met him only a few times, yet I noted his tendency to be irascible. He had a gruff and impatient manner with servants. On one occasion, he became incensed at a remark Bingley made. He imagined an offence where none had been meant."

"Did you relate your opinion to your friend?"

"Yes, we had a heated argument the day I learnt of her engagement. I emphasised the risk of moving to another country with a man she did not know well. But she dismissed my concerns. She grew angry that I did not support her decision, and she stamped away." His arm reached around me, pulling me against him again.

With no will to resist, I laid my head upon his shoulder. "I suppose you saw her again at the wedding feast."

"Yes, we had an amicable, if distant, conversation. Later, I concluded from comments made by Mr. and Mrs. Townshend that they believed my objection to the engagement had arisen from jealousy on my part and regret for not having proposed to her myself. But they were wrong. My concern for her had always been that of a friend."

"Did others draw the same conclusion as Mr. and Mrs. Townshend?" I spoke softly near his ear.

"A few may have, but that was years ago. I assure you that my marriage to an unknown, unrefined country firebrand has been a far more fascinating topic for the London social set." He inched closer, leaving soft, wet kisses around the sensitive area of my neck.

I erupted in giggles. "I hope...they have not been...too disappointed to learn I am civilised and no longer go barefoot in public or eat with my fingers."

"I care not what they think." Fitzwilliam slipped his arm beneath my legs and lifted me. His mouth covered mine in a hungry, intoxicating kiss as he carried me to bed.

Monday, 11 November

I entered the main hall and spotted my husband in the vestibule with a tall, grey-haired stranger. As I neared them, the man looked a bit familiar; perhaps I had observed him at one of the parties we attended last week, but he had not been introduced to me.

"Very well, I shall await you in my coach." The gentleman nodded at Fitzwilliam and departed through the front entrance.

Did my husband intend to leave with him now? My aunt and uncle Gardiner expected us at their home in less than an hour.

Fitzwilliam came to meet me. "Elizabeth, I must speak with you." A knot formed between his brows.

"Of course. Who was that?"

"A friend, Mr. Russell."

Hmm, I had not heard the name before. "Did he bring you bad news?"

"Let us go to the morning room, and I shall explain."

My husband followed me in and closed the door. I went to the sofa, and he sat beside me, taking my hand in his. "I am sorry. I know we had planned to have tea with your aunt and uncle today, but an unexpected business matter has arisen that cannot wait." He raked his fingers through his hair.

"Oh, I see." What sort of 'business matter' would make him so uneasy? It must be serious. I wanted to enquire for details, yet that would be intrusive. He would confide in me in his own time. "May I help in any way?"

"No, thank you. But I should like you to send our regrets to the Gardiners and remain at the house today."

"Why should Georgiana and I not go?"

His thumb brushed over my palm. "An old friend of mine from university is due to arrive today, Mr. Joshua Webb. I apologise for not telling you before now. He wrote last month and informed me of his plans, but it slipped my mind. Years ago, I had...um...offered him a place to stay if he ever came to town. I hope you do not mind."

"No, not at all. I shall be pleased to meet him."

He ran his hand along his lapel. "I may not return before the evening, and I should like you to be here to welcome him."

"Yes, of course."

"I must go now." He did not move, though, and his dark eyes continued to hold mine. "I love you."

Why did he seem so...solemn? I swallowed. "I love you too."

Fitzwilliam gave me an unhurried, sensual kiss that quickened my pulse. He broke away with a sigh. He left a final kiss upon my wrist and left the room.

I shot to my feet and almost ran after him to demand more information. My sense of prudence prevailed, and I remained. Then an image came to me from one morning three months earlier in Ramsgate when Fitzwilliam had been delayed—the 'friend' who had brought him a business proposition had been Mr. Russell. Had he come here today for the same reason? I should press my husband for answers when he returned.

I had just dispatched my note to Aunt Gardiner when Georgiana popped her head in the doorway. "There you are, Elizabeth. Shall we leave soon?"

"No, there has been a change of plans. Fitzwilliam had to leave the house earlier, and he asked that we stay at home. Mr. Webb will arrive today."

"Oh?" Georgiana approached me. "Who is Mr. Webb?"

"He is a friend of Fitzwilliam's from university. Have you never heard your brother mention him?"

"Not that I recall. Have you met him?"

"No. He will stay with us for a while."

"I see." Georgiana glanced at the bracket clock. "Well, I shall be pleased to meet him. In the meantime, I shall go to the music room."

"Very well." I should follow my sister's lead; I needed the practice far more than she did. I entered the hall and went towards my private sitting room to play the instrument there. What sort of man would Mr. Webb turn out to be? With luck, he would be a genial sort like Mr. Bingley.

CHAPTER 5
A Shocking Report

Darcy House

'NONDESCRIPT' SUMMED UP MY INITIAL IMPRESSION OF Mr. Webb. He stood at medium height, with brown hair, a sober demeanour, and average looks.

I apologised for my husband's absence, and he assured me that my presence more than made up for Fitzwilliam's truancy. When he congratulated me on my marriage, a slight smile lightened his mien.

In the drawing-room, Georgiana and I chatted with Mr. Webb over tea. When I asked after his travels, he related his journey from his small estate in Southampton had been satisfactory. At one point, he admired a landscape on the wall opposite him and correctly guessed the artist. I likened him to be similar in personality to my husband—a quiet, intelligent sort, who did not often display emotion and observed a great deal.

When my husband had not come home by four, it made sense to postpone dinner thirty minutes past our usual time and no more; Fitzwilliam had not specified when he would return, so he could be delayed until late in the evening.

I did my best to present a confident comportment when he did not arrive before I announced the meal. Since our marriage, we had always dined together. With his conspicuously empty chair in view, I consumed meagre amounts of food without tasting it. Would he return before I retired for the night?

During the dessert course, Slade entered the dining-parlour and strode towards me. "Pardon me, madam, but Mr. Ellis from the Alien Office is here and has requested an audience with you."

I froze. "Did you say, the *Alien Office*?"

"Yes, madam."

Why would anyone from a Home Office department want to talk to *me*? I placed my napkin on the table. "Thank you, Slade. Please show him to the yellow sitting room."

"Yes, madam." Slade departed.

I met the gazes of Georgiana and Mr. Webb in turn. "Please remain and finish your dessert." I stood, taking care to regulate my voice lest I alarm my sister. "I trust this will not take long."

Mr. Webb rose to his feet. "I believe I ought to accompany you. I do not doubt that if Darcy were here, he would insist upon doing so. Please allow me to provide whatever support I may in his stead."

It would be reassuring to have a friend present. I gave him a grateful smile. "Thank you, I appreciate that."

I glanced at my sister. "We shall see you later in the drawing-room."

"Very well."

Mr. Ellis proved to be a short, stocky gentleman well past forty years of age with dark-brown hair and jowls that quivered with his every move. He met me with a grim expression, responded to my introduction of Mr. Webb with a nod, and insisted I take a seat. I maintained a stiff deportment on the settee facing the officer, with Mr. Webb standing to my right.

The officer removed a small notebook and a pencil from his pocket. "Your butler said your husband was not at home. When did you last see him?"

"I spoke to him before he left the house at around noon."

Mr. Ellis wrote in the notebook. "Did he mention whom he expected to meet or where he was going?"

"No, he did not. He left with another man, a Mr. Russell, but I do not know where they went. He mentioned having a business matter to address."

"Do you know whether they had arranged the meeting ahead of time?"

"No, they had not. We had planned to call upon my aunt and uncle today, but my husband asked me to send our regrets."

"To your knowledge, did Mr. Darcy take a firearm with him?"

A sudden chill incited my shiver. I glanced at Mr. Webb, who remained impassive. In Brighton, Fitzwilliam had taken me to the outskirts of town and instructed me how to handle and fire a small pistol. Once I had demonstrated my facility with the weapon, he admonished me to keep it in my reticule whenever I left the house. He had emphasised the need to take precautions, especially in

London. Our drivers always carried firearms as well. "I am almost certain he did. What is the reason for these questions?"

"I am afraid Mr. Darcy is...missing."

My breath caught in my throat. "*Missing?* What do you mean?"

"At approximately one o'clock today, your husband and Mr. Lewis Russell entered a house in Camberwell, south of the river. Are you well acquainted with Mr. Russell?"

"We have not met, but I glimpsed him today as he was leaving."

"Can you describe him?"

"He is a tall, grey-haired gentleman."

Mr. Ellis nodded. "We have a statement from Mr. Russell's driver. He said that when they arrived at the house in Camberwell, he noticed several other carriages. Mr. Russell sent him to purchase snuff from a tobacconist a few miles away. When he returned, the other coaches were gone. He entered the house and found Mr. Russell and another man. Both had been shot and killed."

Killed? I took a convulsive breath. No, Fitzwilliam could not be dead!

The officer's eyes widened, and he held up his palm. "Oh, excuse me, madam, to be clear, the second man was *not* Mr. Darcy."

Thank God! My hand covered my thundering heart. "Who... um...was the other man?"

"One of my officers identified him as a ne'er-do-well named Evan Leeson. In truth, London is a safer place without him."

"And my husband...he...you did not find him."

"No, madam. We did not detect any sign of him or anyone else. We do not know how many others had been in the house nor their identities."

"Why is the Alien Office involved?"

The officer rubbed his nose. "I am not at liberty to say, madam."

"I suppose I do not care. What matters most now is finding my husband as soon as possible. Whoever shot Mr. Russell may have injured him too." A tremor marred my voice. "Have you searched the area for him?"

"Yes, I had men scour the woods surrounding the house to no avail—dusk came upon us, and we had to cede the effort. We shall return and search again at first light. A couple of my men are questioning the neighbours. Of course, for all we know, Mr. Darcy may have left in one of the other coaches."

A vision of Fitzwilliam bleeding and fleeing through the woods from an armed man flashed in my head. "But he may be hurt and in need of medical care. This cannot wait until morning—we must find him at once!" I shot up from my seat and lurched sideways before steadying myself.

"Try to remain calm, Mrs. Darcy." Mr. Ellis used a soft tone. "I promise you that we shall make every effort to find him. But it would be useless to go now. We should have no hope of finding him until morning."

I curled my hands until my fingernails dug into my palms. He was probably right.

The officer fixed upon Mr. Webb. "Do you have any knowledge of Mr. Darcy's activity today?"

"None whatsoever, I am afraid. He had left before I arrived." Mr. Webb straightened his frame. "I want to accompany you and your men to Camberwell tomorrow and help with the search."

"Very well." Mr. Ellis removed a card from his pocket and handed it to Mr. Webb. "Be at my office by seven." The officer beheld me. "I am sorry to be the bearer of this troubling news. I have men inquiring with the physicians and hospitals in Camberwell. Perhaps one of the others who had been at the house assisted your husband and took him to a medical professional."

"In that case, I should have received word."

"You may yet get a message later this evening. I shall let you know when we learn anything of substance. In all likelihood, Mr. Darcy is on his way home, and it is essential I am notified the moment he returns."

"Yes, of course."

Mr. Ellis's hand brushed over his chin. "You ought to prepare yourself for another possibility: Mr. Darcy may have been taken against his will. This has happened in the past to people known to be wealthy. If this occurred, I should expect you to receive a communication from the culprits with a demand of money in exchange for his release. They may warn you not to seek help from law enforcement. Nevertheless, it is vital that you contact me or one of my fellow officers at once—and tell *no one else*. The fewer people involved, the less likelihood of a complication that could prove dangerous to your husband."

I sucked in my breath. "I understand."

"I shall show myself out." With a bow, Mr. Ellis left the room.

Mr. Webb moved before me. "I expect Darcy will return this evening. However, if he does not, I shall ensure every effort is made to find him tomorrow."

"Thank you. I cannot bear the thought of him being alone and injured out there." I fought back a sob.

His forehead creased. "Try not to fret, Mrs. Darcy. I know my friend—he is smart, agile, and hardy. One way or another, he *will* find his way home."

"Yes, I know he will." I wrapped my arms around my middle. "I shall not say anything to my sister yet."

"Quite right. There is no need to frighten her when it may yet prove unnecessary."

"What am I to do if he does not return, and he is not found tomorrow?"

"I urge you not to distress yourself with possibilities. If you have not heard from him by the time I return tomorrow, we shall plan our next steps then. In the meantime, please ensure you and your sister remain at home."

"Why is that?"

"For one reason, you may be contacted by someone holding Darcy prisoner. For another, it is best to be...cautious." Wrinkles spread from his eyes. "We do not know why those two men were shot. Darcy may have been the intended victim, and if so, others close to him might also be in danger."

I shuddered. "But why would anyone want to hurt him?"

"Any rich man, even a generous and honest one like Darcy, might be deemed an enemy by a dismissed servant or an evicted tenant with a grudge, real or imagined, against him. And a few unscrupulous members of the lower classes justify attacking or stealing from the wealthy because of the advantages the gentry have over them."

"I suppose you are correct. Yes, my sister and I shall remain here."

Mr. Webb leaned closer to me. "Are you well?"

"Yes, I...I think so, thank you." I *must* remain strong for

Georgiana's sake; if Fitzwilliam did not return soon, she would need my support.

"In that case, I shall retire to my room now. I intend to depart early tomorrow. Goodnight."

"Goodnight." When he left, I wandered around the room, distracted by the germ of an idea. Then it came to me: Winston—maybe he could provide insight into where Fitzwilliam might be.

My husband's valet, a fastidious and confident man of perhaps five and thirty, arrived within a minute of my summons. "You wished to see me, Mrs. Darcy?"

I related the known facts of Fitzwilliam's disappearance.

Winston paled and his head dipped—his usual serene deportment shattered. "I am very distressed to hear this. How may I be of assistance?"

"Is there anything you can tell me, any information that might help us find him?"

"No, I am sorry. Nothing like this has ever happened before." He swallowed. "No doubt the master will be home soon. However, if he has not returned by morning, I should like to help search for him."

"What do you propose to do?"

"I should make enquiries at his club and a few other businesses in town to see if anyone has seen him."

"Yes, that would be helpful."

"Very good, madam. You may be assured I shall be discreet and speak only to those whom I know to be trustworthy."

"I appreciate that."

After Winston departed, I collapsed back upon the settee. Several dire circumstances that might have befallen Fitzwilliam tormented me before I banished the thoughts. My husband would return to me. He had become the centre of my life; my heart lived for him. If he had suffered a mortal tragedy, if he no longer lived, I should know it, feel it, sense it—should I not?

Tuesday, 12 November

Last night, I had spent an exhausting two hours with Georgiana affecting a placid tenor. I had explained that Mr. Ellis had asked to speak with Fitzwilliam, and I had informed the investigator that my husband was not at home—a lie of omission though not of substance.

Later in my bed, I had sobbed until the early hours of the morning before finding a short period of fitful sleep. As Gibbs dressed me, I resolved to refrain from succumbing to tears except in the privacy of my chambers. I should appear strong and capable, at least during the day.

With a desire to remain occupied, I spent the morning poring over Fitzwilliam's correspondence. I separated the letters into two stacks: those I should address and those I should set aside for my husband. During our engagement, he had spent several hours reviewing the major points of our marriage contract with me. To my great surprise, he had decreed that if he should ever be absent or incapacitated, I should have control over his business and estate concerns.

The topic had made me uncomfortable; the last thing I wanted to contemplate was a separation from him. Thus, I protested the need for this action. He explained he trusted me above all others, and it gave him peace of mind to ensure no one else could make decisions that affected me or Georgiana.

I had vacillated between pride and apprehension at this revelation; after all, I had never heard of a husband placing so much confidence in his wife. Could his faith in me be misplaced? What if I made a disastrous decision? But Fitzwilliam had assured me that my instincts were sound. He added that I should not go wrong by authorising any course recommended by his steward or solicitor, both of whom had served him faithfully for many years. He had further suggested that, depending on the issue at hand, I may seek the counsel of my uncle or my father.

At noon, Mr. Webb returned to the house and joined me in the study. My shoulders sank at my first sight of him: he entered the room at a weary gait, his aspect glum. I ambled to a seat by the window.

He smoothed his brown hair, taming several blowsy locks, then sat opposite me. "I wish I had better news. Thus far, there has been no sign of Darcy."

My fingers curled around the arms of my chair. "What will Mr. Ellis and his men do now?"

Mr. Webb grimaced. "He would not reveal their plans, but he indicated they would continue to investigate Darcy's disappearance. Mr. Ellis reiterated that he must be notified if we learn anything or if Darcy returns home."

"Where could he be?"

He leaned towards me. "I know not, but I am certain he will be back...soon."

I had been dreading this moment, hoping it would not come. Now I had no choice but to tell Georgiana and notify the family of Fitzwilliam's disappearance.

"Please do not lose hope."

"I have not, but it is—" I flinched at sharp raps upon the door.

"Madam, may I speak to you?" Slade's voice penetrated the dense wood.

"Yes, Slade, enter."

Slade approached me and held out a special edition of The Sun. "I thought you had better see the article on the second page, madam."

"Thank you." I took the periodical.

With a solemn bow, Slade left the room.

I opened the newspaper, and the lower-right section caught my eye: *Wealthy, new-married Derbyshire gentleman missing!* I met Mr. Webb's gaze. "They have revealed Fitzwilliam's disappearance!"

"What does it say?"

I cleared my throat. *"Mr. Fitzwilliam Darcy of Pemberley estate in Derbyshire and Park Lane in London is missing under mysterious circumstances as of Monday, 11 November. He was last seen entering a residence at 5 Flinton Street, Camberwell, in company with Mr. Lewis Russell of Broad Street. The bodies of Mr. Russell and Mr. Evan Leeson, both victims of gunshots, were recovered from the house late yesterday afternoon. The assailant(s) are unknown and at large. According to an official familiar with the matter, Mr. Darcy is not a suspect in the killings. The Alien Office has taken over the investigation. Anyone with information related to this incident is urged to notify the Alien Office on Crown Street."* I set the newspaper on the desk.

"I am sorry, Mrs. Darcy."

I sighed. "The entire town will be speculating on where Fitzwilliam might be." An obscure thought niggled at me. I turned the concept over in my mind until it gained clarity. "Maybe...yes, I believe I could use this development to my advantage." I straightened my spine. "I shall put notices in the major newspapers offering a reward, two hundred pounds, to anyone with information that leads to my husband's safe return."

Mr. Webb cocked his head. "Hmm, that is an...interesting notion. But two hundred pounds is too much—you would have every rogue in the city coming to you with false information in the hopes of it paying off."

"Yet I must offer enough to tempt those who may otherwise be reluctant to reveal what they know."

"I suppose so, but if you insist upon doing this, allow me to meet with those who come forward. Many of them, if not all, are apt to be swindlers, thieves, or worse. I should not want you to be anywhere near them."

"I appreciate your concern, and you are welcome to join me, but I insist upon hearing their statements myself."

He released a veiled groan. "Very well, if you insist."

A hurried set of knocks preceded the door opening again. Slade rushed into the room. "Forgive me, madam, but—"

"This is outrageous!" My husband's cousin Lord Berkeley stormed through the doorway with Lord Matlock a few steps behind him.

"Lord Matlock and Lord Berkeley are here, madam." Slade dipped his chin and shut the door on his way out.

The viscount held a copy of The Sun aloft and thrust it before my face. "We came as soon as we received the paper. Why did you not notify us the moment you learnt of Darcy's disappearance?"

My gaze drifted between Lord Berkeley and his father, the earl. "I had hoped Fitzwilliam would be home by now. I should have sent you a message this afternoon. I did not see the notice in The Sun until moments ago."

The viscount set the newspaper upon a nearby table. "Has Darcy mentioned a need to go to Pemberley or anywhere else?"

"No. He expected to return home last night."

The earl stiffened, and his sight riveted upon Mr. Webb.

"Excuse me, Lord Matlock, Lord Berkeley, may I present Mr. Joshua Webb? He attended Cambridge with Fitzwilliam and is staying with us."

The earl granted Mr. Webb a slight nod. "It is good to meet you."

Mr. Webb bowed. "It is a pleasure to meet you both."

The viscount's eyes narrowed and fixed upon Mr. Webb. "If you have known Darcy since Cambridge, it is odd I never heard your name before. Where are you from?"

"My estate is in Southampton, and I do not often leave the area. This is a rare trip for me."

"And what occasioned this *rare trip*?" Lord Berkeley stepped closer to Mr. Webb.

"My primary object was to see Darcy, but I shall also meet with my solicitor whilst I am here." Mr. Webb maintained an unfettered attitude.

"The timing of your visit is suspicious." Lord Berkeley rolled back upon his heels and shifted towards me. "Mr. Webb ought to find other lodgings until Darcy returns."

I gaped at him. How could he be so rude? "That is not your decision."

"Did Darcy anticipate this visit from his *friend*?"

"Yes. Before he left the house yesterday, my husband mentioned Mr. Webb's expected arrival."

"Still, with the news of Darcy's disappearance spreading through town, I cannot approve of you having a near stranger staying at the house."

With effort, I managed to restrain myself from making a rash retort; my vitriol would do no good and would provide the presumptuous man more fodder for his censure. Thank goodness I did not need his approval. To think that upon my initial sight of Lord Berkeley, I had deemed him to be the spitting image of my husband. But once the viscount had opened his mouth to speak, his overt arrogance revealed him to belong to a separate, singular category. Fitzwilliam had made his opinion of his eldest cousin clear: he tolerated the viscount, after all, one had little alternative with family, but considered him to be far inferior in every significant way to his younger brother, Colonel Richard Fitzwilliam. I had yet to meet the colonel, who had been sent to Spain earlier this year.

I raised upon my toes to gain a bit of height. "In fact, I am grateful for the assistance Mr. Webb has provided. He met with an investigator from the Alien Office earlier today and joined in the search they conducted." I related the circumstances of Fitzwilliam's departure yesterday, Mr. Ellis's alarming report, and my decision to run newspaper advertisements.

Lord Matlock moved before me. "If you offer an award for information, you will be inviting trouble."

In the corner of my eye, I caught a glimpse of Mr. Webb's subtle nod. "I have been forewarned of the possible dangers, but I am determined to do everything possible to help bring Fitzwilliam home. Someone may have seen him or may know where to find him."

"Does Georgiana know he is missing yet?" The earl used a low voice.

"No, I shall inform her shortly."

"The poor girl will be inconsolable." Lord Matlock rubbed the nape of his neck. "It occurs to me that she may feel more comfortable staying with family. That is to say, she may prefer to be with her aunt and uncle during this trying time." The earl had the decency to blush at his faux pas. "When you speak to her, please let her know we should love to have her with us."

I bit my tongue as a reminder to maintain a tranquil temper. "I shall, thank you."

The earl nodded. "And, of course, if we may assist you in any way, do not hesitate to ask."

"I appreciate that."

The viscount strutted towards the desk and scoured the surface. He lifted the letter atop of a stack—the one from Mr. Rutley, the butler at Pemberley. He came towards me, waving the missive. "Based upon the date of this letter, it could not have arrived before today. How dare you invade Darcy's privacy by opening his personal correspondence?"

"My husband made his wishes clear to me, his solicitor, and his servants—he designated me to carry on in his stead at any time he is not at hand."

"He did *what?*" The viscount's voice gained volume. "That is absurd! Why would any man want his wife to read through his private letters?"

Mr. Webb shifted closer to me. His jaw clenched, and a fierce glint flickered in his eyes.

"I did not open *all* of Fitzwilliam's correspondence." I employed a swift cadence. "He intended for me to open any post sent by a business or from a list of people he provided whose letters merited immediate attention. I left the remainder for his perusal."

The viscount tramped back to the desk and threw the letter upon it. "When I next see Darcy, I shall convince him to put an end to this...irregular practice."

The earl and viscount soon took their leave, an event that coincided with Mr. Webb's transition to a less rigid deportment.

Mr. Webb moved opposite me. "If you are certain you want to go forward with your advertisements, will you allow me to contact *The Morning Post* and *The Morning Chronicle* on your behalf?" He glanced at the mantle clock. "I could go to the papers directly and ensure the notices appear in tomorrow's editions."

"Yes, I should appreciate that."

We reviewed the wording for the reward offer before he left.

The distant sound of Rory's bark drew my sight to the window. I passed through the panelled-glass door to the garden and took the stone path towards my dog. Rory jerked his head up, barked again, and ran to me. I crouched to pat him and waved at Martin, one of our footmen, who stood in the distance. "I shall watch over Rory for a while."

"Yes, madam." With a bow, Martin set off towards the servants' entrance. Rory and I wound through the circuit of trails throughout the garden until we had trodden the same ground many times over, and a portion of my restlessness had abated. We entered the door to the study, and Rory scampered to the area behind Fitzwilliam's desk. He sniffed at my husband's chair and wandered round it. He halted and looked at me, whining.

"He is not here, but he will be home soon." I heaved a deep breath. I could put off telling Georgiana the bad news no longer. "Come on, boy, let us go and find my sister."

Rory and I joined Georgiana in her private sitting room. I sat with her on the sofa and held her hand. Rory lay on the floor between us with his head atop my slipper and his haunch against my sister's leg. I told her everything—all the known facts of Fitzwilliam's disappearance. I made an effort to conceal my anxiety, emphasising my belief that we should see him soon. In conclusion, I related Lord Matlock's suggestion that she stay at his home. Surely, she would not want to go!

"I much prefer to remain here with you."

I gathered Georgiana in my arms, stroking her back. "Thank you, dearest. I appreciate that."

She clung to me and snuffled. "My aunt and uncle cannot make me stay with them, can they?"

"No, they cannot." Once her breathing calmed, I drew back.

Georgiana's lower lip trembled. "I hate to say this, but I do not understand. How...um...can you be certain Fitzwilliam will be well? He might be badly injured or...or worse."

I met her teary, blue eyes and sought a collected air. "I cannot be *absolutely* certain. Yet I believe he will return to us—it must be so. Otherwise, I expect my intuition would have forewarned me—with a...a foreboding."

"But there is no logical reason to think that—even though I want to believe you—unless you have had previous premonitions that came true."

"No, I have not. Nevertheless, I refuse to countenance any other conclusion—not until I am forced to do so."

She nodded. "I shall try to maintain a hopeful outlook." She knelt to brush her hand along Rory's neck. "May I keep him here for a while?"

"Yes, of course." I kissed her forehead, left the room, and went downstairs. Despite my disinclination to put faith in anything coming from Lord Berkeley, his unveiled suspicion of Mr. Webb lingered on my mind. How well did Fitzwilliam really know this 'old friend'? I came upon Slade, and I called out to him.

"Yes, madam?"

"You have worked for the Darcys for several decades, have you not?"

"I am privileged to have been in the family's employ for more than forty years."

"Had you ever seen Mr. Webb before he arrived yesterday?"

"No, I had not."

"Had you ever heard Mr. Darcy mention his name before?"

"I do not believe so."

"Which guest room is he using?"

"The blue chamber on the second floor—the one nearest the sitting room."

"Thank you." I returned to the stairs. Maybe the viscount had unduly influenced me to be wary of Mr. Webb, but I needed to assure myself, if possible, of his trustworthiness. At the second-floor landing, I went towards his guest room and entered, closing the door behind me. I hastened to the chest of drawers and searched through it as quickly as possible whilst attempting to be quiet. The sound of footsteps in the hall made me flinch and hold still, but they continued onwards. I remained braced for a maid or Mr. Webb's valet to walk in and find me prying into my guest's personal items. What could I say in my defence if that occurred?

The escritoire held nothing of interest. I knelt before the decorative trunk at the foot of the bed. Beneath a stack of trousers and breeches I found a small valise. I lifted the luggage out, placed it on the floor, and attempted to open it, but it was locked. I removed one of my hairpins and used it to poke at the lock. After two minutes of my efforts, the case clicked open. Inside, I found several books: a volume on military history, a treatise by a popular philosopher, and a French/English dictionary. Tucked between the pages of the dictionary, I discovered an unsealed letter addressed simply to 'Mr. Vane'. I unfolded it and read the missive.

Vane,
The address you seek is 40 Woburn Place.
J.D.

What did this mean? Did Mr. Webb stay at my house or Mr. Vane? I returned to the escritoire, found a small piece of paper, and copied the brief message.

I refolded the note to Mr. Vane and put everything back as it had been. Upon entering the hall without being seen, I released a heavy breath and continued to my chamber, shaking the paper to dry the ink. I reposed on the sofa and stared at my written words. What, if anything, should I do with this information? I could not query Mr. Webb without revealing I had searched his room. For now, I must bide my time and remain alert for any suspicious behaviour. Nothing mattered more than finding my husband, and as long as Mr. Webb offered his assistance to that end, I should accept it.

I lowered my head, burying my face in my hands. *Oh, Fitzwilliam, where are you? Please come home to me!*

In the late afternoon, Winston returned to the house. The dejected valet reported that no one he had spoken to had seen Fitzwilliam. I thanked him for his efforts.

Georgiana, Mr. Webb, and I shared a quiet dinner during which we all picked at our food. In an effort to keep my hands occupied, I carved my portion of chicken into countless tiny pieces.

Throughout the first course, I maintained a covert observation of Mr. Webb, as though to divine a clue to his true character. Since his arrival, I had been so engrossed by Fitzwilliam's absence, and later his disappearance, that I had never asked my guest any personal questions.

In light of the mysterious message I had discovered in his room, it seemed prudent to press him for details. "Mr. Webb, I have been remiss before now. I have never asked you about your home in Southampton."

"Under the circumstances, it is understandable. My life is rather dull, so I have little to tell. My estate is small. Our current primary crops are turnips, and we breed carriage horses."

"Do you have a large family?"

"No, I have no brothers or sisters."

"That is a shame."

"Yes, my late mother suffered through several miscarriages and never had another child. My parents have been deceased these past six years—they perished in a carriage accident."

"Oh dear. I am sorry to hear that."

"That is very sad." Georgiana gave him a sympathetic look.

"I appreciate that."

"Is there a Mrs. Webb back home at your estate?" I swallowed a tiny sip of ale.

"No. Thus far, I have evaded the parson's mousetrap." His mouth softened, hinting at a smile.

"It seems you are pleased with your status. Still, one day you might stumble upon the path of Cupid's arrow, perhaps when you least expect it, and your outlook on marriage may change."

He raised his glass to me. "Your point is taken, madam."

After the meal, Mr. Webb declared a desire to retire to his room, and he bid us goodnight. Georgiana and I practised a duet in the music room until I caught her in a yawn and urged her to retire. I accompanied her to her chamber and proceeded to my room. Restless and wide awake, I eschewed my bed and settled by the fireplace with a glass of wine and Rory at my feet. How could I face another night alone?

Perhaps an hour had passed, my wine glass drained, when Slade came to inform me my aunt and uncle Gardiner called. *Dear me*, I had completely forgotten to notify them of Fitzwilliam's disappearance! I ran downstairs and burst into the sitting room. My aunt and uncle rushed to me and held me from either side.

Uncle Gardiner rested his chin atop my head. "My dear Lizzy, forgive us for arriving at this late hour. When we saw the newspaper, we had to see you tonight."

"I am glad you are here, and I am sorry for not writing to you."

"Nay, do not give that a thought." My aunt's soothing voice surrounded me like a downy blanket.

"I feel as though I am caught in a horrible dream from which there is no escape. It terrifies me to think I might never see my husband again, and yet I must be strong and put on a brave front for those who depend upon me. And I refuse to give fodder to those who are keen to be my detractors."

"You are human, my dear." Aunt Gardiner ran her hand in a rhythmic pattern over my back. "You need not be afraid to show it."

"I doubt Lady Matlock would agree with you."

My aunt and uncle released me. Aunt Gardiner's palm caressed my cheek. "Has the countess been unkind to you?"

"No, I should not say so. Although it is clear she is not happy that Fitzwilliam married me, she has been helpful. It has been...challenging at times to adjust to my new life, but it is nothing I cannot handle."

We took seats together, and I recounted all that had taken place—including my discovery in Mr. Webb's room. I trusted their judgment above anyone else's save Fitzwilliam's.

Uncle Gardiner scowled. "If your guest is an imposter, then he could be a dangerous man. The safest choice would be to ask Mr. Webb, or whoever he is, to leave. And I want to be there when you speak to him."

"I understand why you would suggest that, but I am not inclined to take such a drastic action. The message I found could have an innocuous explanation. Thus far, Mr. Webb has been helpful to me. Besides, Fitzwilliam did tell me to await him."

His brows shifted up. "The fact that Mr. Darcy expected his friend's visit does not negate the possibility that the man calling himself Mr. Webb could be a fraud. Maybe a misfortune befell the real Mr. Webb, and this person took his place."

"That sounds so...fantastical. If Mr. Webb wished to do me harm, he has had ample opportunities already—instead, he has been supportive, even protective. I have not noticed anything in his conduct to make me wary of him. Besides, I have a houseful of servants to protect me, several of whom are skilled marksmen. In addition, I have my own pistol now."

"*You* have a pistol?" My uncle shared a look with Aunt Gardiner. "I have never known you to handle a firearm."

"Fitzwilliam taught me how to use it during our stay in Brighton. We spent many hours practising before he deemed me proficient. He admonished me never to leave the house without the pistol in town."

"Well, I suppose in London one cannot be too careful."

Aunt Gardiner met my gaze. "How has Miss Darcy taken your husband's disappearance?"

"I broke the news to her today. She is frightened and upset."

My aunt turned to my uncle. "Maybe Mr. Notley can be of service. Do you not think he may be able to find Mr. Darcy?"

"Yes, Modesty, that is a fine idea." He moved to the edge of his seat, facing me. "Last spring, I had a series of thefts from the warehouse. I hired Mr. Jeremy Notley, a Bow Street Runner, to investigate, and he identified the thief among my employees within two days. I could ask him to look into Mr. Darcy's disappearance and also verify Mr. Webb's identity. What do you think, Lizzy? Should I retain Mr. Notley?"

"Yes, thank you." I reached into my pocket and removed the note I had written earlier. "Here is the information I copied. Perchance Mr. Vane is a friend of Mr. Webb's who had asked this 'JD' person for the address on Mr. Webb's behalf."

"Yes, it is possible." Uncle Gardiner took my offering and gave it a glance before folding the paper and tucking it in his coat pocket. "Very well, Lizzy, I shall speak to Mr. Notley tomorrow."

"I appreciate your help. Maybe this Bow Street Runner will succeed where the Alien Office, at least so far, has failed."

CHAPTER 6

Facing Friends, Family, and Others

Wednesday, 13 November
Darcy House

I JERKED AWAKE. "FITZWILLIAM." MY WHISPERED CALL seemed to echo throughout the dark chamber as though to taunt me. My hand reached out to his side of the bed, finding the sheets cold and empty. Reality engulfed me with a jolt—I had been dreaming of him again.

Moisture filled my eyes. I grabbed the handkerchief on the bedside table and dabbed at escaping tears. Despite the extra blankets on my bed, I shivered. Without my husband's embrace, I may never again know true warmth and comfort. Unless—until—he returned, the only solace I found might be in dreams.

A soft whine drew my attention. In the dim moonlight, I could make out Rory's faint form; he stood on his hind legs, peeking at me with his furry front paws braced upon the bed-clothes. My dog had been sleeping on a soft rug a few feet away. I moved closer and patted him. "I did not mean to disturb you, boy. Go back to sleep." I gently pushed him backwards until his front paws landed on the floor. I reclined and pulled the blankets over me, closing my weary eyes. Maybe by focusing upon pleasant memories, I could escape into another dream for a few precious hours.

"You must eat, you poor dear, or you will waste away." Lady Gillingham pointed to my plate, which I had filled but not touched.

I glanced at Priscilla, who lay stretched out upon my lap in a lazy position, and brushed my fingers along the cat's back with soft strokes. "I appreciate your concern. At the moment, though, I lack an appetite."

Lady Gillingham shook her head. "Nevertheless, you must eat a little. I insist upon it. After all, you would not want Mr. Darcy to return to an ill wife."

I forced a smile—she meant well. "No, certainly not." I picked up the least offensive item on my plate, a biscuit, and took a tiny bite. I chewed for an inordinate amount of time and needed a mouthful of tea to swallow the morsel.

"Ah, that is better, is it not?"

I nodded and dabbed a napkin at the corner of my mouth.

Lines filled Lady Gillingham's brow. "Now then, I strongly advise you to avoid reading *The Morning Post* or any of the papers for the next week or so. I fear they will continue to print wild speculation with regard to Mr. Darcy until they fix upon their next big story."

"I must be one of the few people in town who is not reading them."

"Pray, do not fret over the gossip. It is inevitable in a situation like this, but their talk will fade to nothing once your husband returns. And no matter what happens, you may count upon my full support."

"That is exceedingly kind of you."

Lady Gillingham lifted her hand in a dismissive wave. "Nonsense, it is the least I can do. I cannot imagine what you are going through. You, a new-married young lady, separated from your husband with no idea of his whereabouts and no indication of when he will return. It is a wonder you can leave your bed. Mind you, I never marked you for a delicate sort. Rather, I fancy you are capable of handling whatever comes your way."

"I hope you are correct."

"Of course I am." Her gaze lowered to my lap. "You know, you are one of the few people whom Priscilla allows to hold her. It is obvious she is comfortable with you. If I did not know better, I might suspect she prefers you to me." Lady Gillingham's lips curled into a crooked smile.

"No, Priscilla merely recognises my affinity for animals. Back in Hertfordshire, I had several feline friends."

"Ah, that makes sense."

Slade entered the room. "Pardon me, madam, but Mr. Haddington is here to see you."

"Ah...well..." My sight drifted to Lady Gillingham. Would she object to his presence? I searched my mind for anything Fitzwilliam or Lady Matlock may have mentioned to reveal the lady's opinion of Mr. Haddington without success. To my good fortune, she smiled.

"By all means, Mrs. Darcy, let him join us." Lady Gillingham used a bright tone. "Priscilla has always overlooked the man, which means he is unremarkable but not a bad sort."

With a heavy exhalation, I shifted to address Slade. "Please show him in."

Mr. Haddington entered the room with a stricken expression. "I hope you will pardon my intrusion, Mrs. Darcy, Lady Gillingham."

"Not at all, Mr. Haddington." I pointed to a chair. "Will you not sit?"

"No, thank you. I shall not stay long. I was shocked to hear of Darcy's disappearance and wanted to offer my condolences. If there is anything, anything at all, I may do to assist you, I am at your disposal."

"Thank you very much. I appreciate that." I smiled upon Mr. Haddington. He had a long-standing friendship with Fitzwilliam; did he know my house guest? "We have one of my husband's friends staying with us—a Mr. Webb. He has been most helpful during this trying time. Have you ever met him?"

"Mr. Webb?" Mr. Haddington tilted his head. "No, I am afraid not."

Earlier, Mr. Webb and I had intended to meet with a man who professed to have knowledge of Fitzwilliam's location. When Lady Gillingham arrived, Mr. Webb urged me to go and receive her. Once I had obtained his promise to provide a full report of the man's statement, I left him. "He is occupied at the moment, or I should introduce you."

"Perhaps another time." After a few more minutes of conversation, Mr. Haddington took his leave.

I poured more tea into Lady Gillingham's cup. "It was kind of Mr. Haddington to call."

"Hmm, yes. Of course, that man owes a great deal to your husband. After the trouble Lord Carswell brought upon the family, Mr. Darcy exerted himself to ensure Mr. Haddington's continued entree into several of the most exclusive homes in London—he has been Mr. Haddington's best advocate."

"Well, I am glad to know my husband has loyal friends in town."

"He does indeed." Lady Gillingham took a bite of lemon cake. "I do hope Mr. Haddington will find himself a wife—it would do him a world of good. I believe enough time has passed since that business with the eldest Weston daughter. Did Mr. Darcy ever tell you that sad tale?"

"No, he did not."

"Well, the former Miss Weston is the eldest daughter of a wealthy landowner from Lincolnshire. Mr. Weston brought his family to London for Miss Weston's debut Season. Mr. Haddington fell in love with the young lady, and the pair became betrothed. A few weeks before the wedding, Lord Carswell was arrested for treason. Mr. Weston ended the engagement and took his daughter home to Lincolnshire. Soon thereafter, she married a gentleman from a neighbouring estate."

I set my teacup upon my saucer with a clang. "Oh dear, poor Mr. Haddington—he must have been anguished!"

"Yes, without a doubt. For months he refused to leave his house, drowning his sorrows in liquor. It is due to your husband that he ever emerged from that melancholy. For a while, the man appeared to be determined to drink himself to death. Mr. Darcy, though, refused to give up on his friend, and in time, his persistence paid off."

"I have noted a dolefulness to Mr. Haddington's comportment, and I attributed it to his being shunned in public by former friends. Now, I suspect his lost love may be the primary reason. Unless I am mistaken, he is not yet ready to open his heart to another."

"Alas, I think you may be correct."

Once Lady Gillingham had departed, I entered the garden to dust Priscilla's white hairs off my gown, then proceeded to Georgiana's sitting room.

My sister opened the door to me, her blue eyes tinged with red. "Is there any news?"

"No, not yet." My arms encircled her, and she rested her head on my shoulder.

"Since the reward notice appeared in the paper, I imagine you will attract many responses. Maybe we shall find Fitzwilliam today."

I drew back to face her. "I hope so. We had a man this morning who thought he saw Fitzwilliam at the docks yesterday. Winston and Martin went to make enquiries. Mr. Webb met with a second man whilst I sat with Lady Gillingham."

"I saw her arrive earlier. I do not know how you do it." Georgiana's brows lowered. "You are answering Fitzwilliam's correspondence and taking calls. I know you are fretting over my brother as much or even more than I am, yet you *appear* to be so calm and...capable."

My gaze averted towards the window, and I blinked at a welling of tears. "It would not do for me to shirk my responsibilities. Besides, I should feel even worse if I did not keep busy. As long as I have faith he will return, I can endure this."

Georgiana took my hand and squeezed it. "I am so grateful you are my sister. If you can be strong, I can be too."

I smiled upon her. "And I am *very* glad you chose to remain here with me."

The sounds of voices led me to the front of the house. In the vestibule, Slade took Lady Matlock's hat and coat. I went to meet her. "Good day, Lady Matlock. Shall we have tea in the drawing-room?"

"No, thank you. I shall not remain long. I presume you have had no word from Darcy or you would have apprised us."

"That is correct."

The countess wrung her hands. "I am bewildered by his disappearance. For this to have happened to my nephew is unimaginable. He is one of the most responsible men I know." She pointed to the nearby sitting room. "Let us go in here."

I followed Lady Matlock into the room and sat across from her.

Her eyes narrowed into a piercing glare. "Did the two of you quarrel before he left?"

My hand curled upon the pillow beside me. What did she think —that he would stay away to avoid me, leaving his loved ones to fret for him, because of a marital altercation? How ridiculous! "No, not at all."

"Have you...um..." The countess coughed and lowered her voice. "Have you been submitting to your husband as a good wife ought to do?"

I drew to an erect posture. "Fitzwilliam and I have a happy marriage, and I shall not discuss the matter any further."

After a long moment, Lady Matlock gave me a brisk nod. "I thought as much, but under the circumstances, it seemed prudent to ask. If you can manage it, I suggest you continue to see a select number of callers—many will wish to offer their support, and they will help to dispute the tattle spreading through town." Her mouth flattened. "Of course, a few others who call will hope to find you distressed and despondent. If you choose to see them, do not give them the satisfaction."

"I shall not."

"Did you receive any callers today?"

"I saw Lady Gillingham earlier and Mrs. Stapleton before that. Both ladies have been most kind. Oh, and Mr. Haddington came to offer his assistance as well."

She released a sigh. "I hate to say it, but *that* man's support will not benefit you—the reverse is true."

"Nevertheless, I am grateful for his offer."

"My husband told me that you are handling Darcy's business matters. I caution you to let as few people as possible know this—it is unorthodox, to say the least."

"I understand."

Lady Matlock cleared her throat. "I realise now that I was wrong to think Darcy had erred in choosing you as his wife. I ought to have known that he, of all people, would not make a frivolous choice in a matter as vital as marriage. Since your arrival in London, you have proceeded with tact, kindness, and intelligence. You are good for my nephew and for my niece as well. I apologise for having misjudged you."

This concession, though extraordinary, failed to move me as perhaps it ought to have done. No doubt if this moment had arrived at a less chaotic time, I could appreciate it more. "I am pleased to accept your apology, my lady, and I appreciate everything you have done to help me."

"You are welcome." The countess left me to have a quick word with Georgiana before returning home.

Mr. Webb came to the sitting room. "Ah, there you are, Mrs. Darcy. The most recent respondent to your advertisement was the most useless one yet. He was a vagrant with no information to share. He came to spout his hatred of the gentry, whom he blames for ruining his life. I am glad you were spared his vitriol."

"It is a shame he wasted your time."

"Unless you have need of me at the moment, I intend to walk the grounds and surrounding areas to ensure no one is loitering near the premises."

"By all means, please do."

With a nod, he departed.

I should have gone to the study, but I encountered Slade, who informed me that Mrs. Fraser and Miss Townshend called.

Last Thursday, we had dined at the Townshend home. I had scrutinised every interaction between Fitzwilliam and Mrs. Fraser for hints of an abiding flame, but both had been models of platonic amity. For her part, Mrs. Fraser had paid far more attention to *me*; she appeared genuine in her expressed desire to be my friend.

I joined the two ladies in the morning room.

Mrs. Fraser rushed towards me, her forehead fraught with lines. "Please excuse us for imposing upon you at such a difficult time, Mrs. Darcy."

I pressed my lips into a weak smile. "Nonsense. It is a pleasure to see you, Mrs. Fraser"—I met the younger sister's gaze—"and Miss Townshend. Please, sit, and I shall order tea."

"No, pray do not bother." Mrs. Fraser held her hand up. "We do not want to trouble you, and we shall not take up much of your time. We came to express our deepest sympathy for you and Georgiana. We, my entire family, are distraught over Mr. Darcy's disappearance. I do not suppose you have heard from him or have any news?"

I stared into her sombre, dark eyes. Did her concern indicate a sentiment stronger than friendship? I could not be certain. "No, I have not."

"Our parents are beside themselves." Miss Townshend used a soft tone.

"Indeed, yes." Mrs. Fraser touched her sister's shoulder. "They have tasked us to convey their offer to provide any assistance you may need. Is there anything we can do for you now?"

"I thank you, no. But I appreciate your family's offer very much. The kindness from Fitzwilliam's friends has been gratifying. Please thank your parents for me."

"Yes, I shall do that." Mrs. Fraser took Miss Townshend's arm. "We shall leave you now."

After the ladies' coach had entered the next street, I went out of the front door and lingered on the portico, allowing the crisp breeze to revive me. I skimmed the area and found it empty. Well, not quite —a tall, dark-haired man sat on the bench near the entrance to Hyde Park reading a newspaper. Based upon his attire, he might be a clerk or tradesman. He wore spectacles and had a full beard. He had every right to be there, and I had no reason to be suspicious of him. Still, if anyone wished to watch the front of the house, that bench made an ideal spot for it.

Movement in Hyde Park caught my attention: a pair of gentlemen passed by on horseback at a leisurely pace. Tomorrow morning, I should take a long walk in the park. Two days without my usual exercise had left me out of sorts and fidgety.

A fine coach entered the street and stopped before the house. Why did the crest look familiar? The carriage door opened, and a dapper, chestnut-haired gentleman alighted—*Mr. Bingley!* He reached in and handed my beloved elder sister from the vehicle.

"Jane!" I raced down the steps.

My beautiful, blonde sister opened her arms for me. "Oh, Lizzy, it is so good to see you! I have been concerned for you."

We held each other, swaying from side to side. I broke my grip to wipe away tears.

Mr. Bingley patted my arm. "Mrs. Darcy, it is a great pleasure to see you, though I am very sorry for the circumstances."

I raised my head from Jane's shoulder. "Thank you, Mr. Bingley. I am glad to see you too." Then movement beyond him caught my eye: my dear father emerged from the coach. *Papa is here!*

He came towards me. "Lizzy, I hope you do not mind this impromptu imposition."

I released my sister and ran into his waiting arms. "Oh, Papa. You could never be an imposition." With a sudden consciousness of our public position, I stepped back from him. Although my father looked as robust as ever, the wrinkles beneath his eyes appeared deeper than when we last met. "Please, let us go into the house. We shall talk over refreshments."

In the drawing room, I poured tea for Mr. Bingley, Jane, and Papa.

My father arched his bushy, grey eyebrows. "Now, Lizzy, we do not want to put you to any trouble. We are happy to stay with the Gardiners if—"

"Perish the thought! Let us have no more talk of you staying elsewhere—of course you will remain here. I want to spend as much time with you as possible."

"As you wish, my dear." Papa reposed against his chair, offering a wry smile. "At any rate, you may count on us getting out of your way tomorrow."

"I think you know I should love to have you stay longer."

"Even so, I shall have had more than enough of London by then. Besides, your mother took to her bed when she learnt Mr. Darcy is missing. She wanted Jane to remain and comfort her, so she will be on tenterhooks until we return."

"I understand." My sight drifted to Mr. Bingley. "You will stay the night too, I hope."

"That is most kind of you, but I must decline. My brother's home is nearby, and he is expecting me. Besides, it would not be proper for me to stay in the same home as my...um...that is to say..."

Mr. Bingley turned to Jane, and a coral shade imbued his complexion. "Pardon me, but I have made a bungle of this."

Jane touched his hand. "It is of no moment—I should have told Lizzy the news myself soon enough." She beamed at me. "Charles and I are engaged."

I launched forwards to give her a hug. "I am so happy for you—for both of you."

"Thank you, dear Lizzy."

I grinned at Mr. Bingley. "Congratulations!"

He shook my proffered hand. "I appreciate that. I could not be more pleased that Darcy will be my brother, and you my sister."

Jane's smile receded. "Of course, we cannot be completely content until Mr. Darcy returns home."

"Yes, quite right." Mr. Bingley assumed a rigid bearing. "I had thought, with your agreement, that whilst I am in town, I should hire a man to search for Darcy."

"Thank you. I appreciate your kind offer very much, but Uncle Gardiner is retaining a Bow Street Runner whom he has employed in the past. And the Alien Office is investigating Fitzwilliam's disappearance as well, or so they say."

With an uncharacteristic frown, Mr. Bingley tipped his head to the side. "Do you doubt the Alien Office is trying to find Darcy?"

"It is difficult to know what to think. On Monday evening, one of their officers informed me that Fitzwilliam was missing, but I have had no word from them since then. I have placed a reward advertisement in the paper for anyone with information leading to his return."

Papa adjusted his spectacles to the bridge of his nose. "I understand why you chose to take that step, and it could prove to be a fruitful plan. Yet it may also attract the worst rascals in town. I urge you to take all due precautions with anyone who responds to the notice."

"Yes, I am being careful. And you will be glad to know a guest is staying with us, a friend of Fitzwilliam's, Mr. Joshua Webb."

"Indeed?" My father tasted his tea. "Well, I am in anticipation of meeting him."

I omitted any mention of my suspicion towards Mr. Webb. After all, he continued to provide valuable support to me. And as time went on, I grew all the more certain he could be trusted.

I passed a dish of potatoes to my future brother-in-law, seated to my right, and it occurred to me that he and Fitzwilliam had gone to the same university. "Ah, Mr. Bingley, I neglected to mention earlier that Mr. Webb also attended Cambridge." I kept Mr. Webb within my peripheral vision. "Perhaps the two of you have crossed paths before."

"I do not believe so." Mr. Bingley eyed Mr. Webb. "I should have remembered if we had."

With no outward sign of unease, Mr. Webb turned to Mr. Bingley. "I am certain we never met before today. When did you arrive at Cambridge?"

"I began my studies in the year seven."

"Well, that explains it—I finished mine in the year six."

A commotion in the outer hall drew my attention. Moments later, a distinctively dissonant female voice screeched an unintelligible demand, leaving me in no doubt of her identity. Good Lord, what did Lady Catherine want? I almost choked on the morsel I had been chewing, and a fit of queasiness suppressed any remaining appetite I may have had.

Slade strode into the room with my husband's aunt close upon his heels. "Forgive me, madam, but Lady Catherine insisted upon seeing you at once."

"I demand a private audience with you this minute, Miss Bennet!" She sneered at me. "This is a vital matter that cannot wait."

The gentlemen at the table stood before the spectacle of a tall, well-dressed elderly lady in high dudgeon and devoid of civility. Jane appeared to be frozen in shock, whilst Georgiana bowed her head.

I rose to my feet. "Please excuse me." I left the dining-parlour and marched to the sitting room at the other end of the house; I should at least spare those at the dinner table from further exposure to Lady Catherine's hostility and boorishness. My husband's aunt followed, pounding her walking stick on the floor with a ferocious rhythm.

Once I had closed the sitting room door, I confronted her. "You ought to be ashamed of yourself—I have never witnessed a worse breach of etiquette!"

Lady Catherine's eyes bulged in an alarming manner, as though they might flee their sockets. "How dare you? You have no right to address me with such insolence! You, with your plebeian origins and woeful lack of education. God only knows what a detrimental influence you have already wrought upon my poor niece. Darcy's disappearance is *your* fault. If not for you, if you had not tricked him into marrying you, he would have no reason to go out gallivanting. He would be at home where he belongs!"

"That is an absurd and insulting insinuation." I pressed a hand against my gurgling abdomen. "Fitzwilliam would never abandon his family and his responsibilities, leaving us concerned for his welfare. He is far too honourable to do anything of the sort. A misfortune has befallen him—I know not what. But I do know he would be here if he could. And he *will* return as soon as he is able."

"Oh balderdash!" Spittle disgorged from Lady Catherine's mouth, inducing me to step backwards. "He left because of *you*. He came to his senses and realised the disastrous mistake he had made in marrying you, just as I knew he would. He must be despondent at the thought of being bound to you for the remainder of his life, but it need not be the case. With your cooperation, he may obtain an annulment. Give me your agreement, and I shall see that you are well rewarded."

Was she mad or just ignorant? "My husband does not regret our marriage, and even if he did, there are no grounds for an annulment."

"There could be grounds. All you need to do is say you defrauded him. You could provide a written statement declaring you had told Darcy you had a dowry of ten thousand pounds. Since it is untrue, it would be grounds for an annulment."

"That is absurd."

"It will succeed as long as *you* are willing to do what is necessary to set him free." Her arm flounced in my direction. "Afterwards, I should secure your future. Mr. Collins, my rector and your father's heir presumptive, is not yet married. One word from me and he will propose to you—you will be mistress of your family's estate."

My father had delighted in showing me the ridiculous letter he received from Mr. Collins in the first week of September. His cousin urged him to disallow my marriage as his benefactress deemed me an unsuitable wife for her eminent nephew. Although we had never met the man, his wording demonstrated his ignorant and pompous nature. "My husband loves me. An annulment is the last thing he would want."

With a baleful camber to her lips, she barked out a laugh. "If you believe that, you are not as clever as I had imagined. Do you pretend not to know what most of the *ton* has already deduced? Darcy has not returned to you because he has found solace in the arms of another woman."

"That is a vicious lie!"

"It is the truth, and the sooner you accept it, the better it will be for everyone. I do not know whom he is with, but there are two obvious possibilities. Many are speculating that he returned to his former paramour, Miss Comerford." A malicious grin contorted Lady Catherine's face. "But I should wager he is with his first love, Mrs. Fraser, who recently returned to England. I imagine he leased a house in town so she can meet him there whilst being close to the Townshends' home where their child resides."

My throat constricted. *Their child?*

"I see from your expression you had no idea he had fathered that young girl of hers. I had not concluded the truth until last week, when I called upon Mrs. Townshend, and she had the nurse bring out her granddaughter. The little girl bears a close likeness to Darcy. She has jet-black curly hair—a trait not shared by anyone on her mother's side of the family. You would not know this, but the late Mr. Fraser had flaxen hair, a shade lighter than Mrs. Fraser's locks. And I noted at the time that the baby arrived *fewer than eight months* after the Frasers' marriage."

"That is a wicked and disgusting accusation. You have impugned the characters of both your nephew and Mrs. Fraser. Besides, it makes little sense. If they had been in love years ago, they would have married. Instead, she wed Mr. Fraser."

"Matters of the heart are not always straightforward. I presume they had a lovers' squabble. Mrs. Fraser is known to have a fiery temper. Soon thereafter, she made the impulsive decision to accept Mr. Fraser's proposal. She may not have realised her delicate condition until later. No doubt she repented in leisure for her impetuosity."

No, I did not believe it! Yet I had not known Fitzwilliam then. Could he have altered in the last several years? Or...did I not comprehend his nature as well as I had supposed? Whilst I fought my body's inclination to wilt, I lacked the fortitude to form a suitable retort.

Lady Catherine leaned upon her walking stick. "Now that Mr. Fraser is deceased and Mrs. Fraser is back in England, *you* are the only obstacle between my nephew and his true love, the mother of his child. Now, will you agree to set Darcy free?"

My power of speech returned with a vengeance. "No, I will never be party to your vile scheme. And this is the last time you will insult me in my home." I rang for Slade, and he appeared within seconds.

"Yes, madam."

"Lady Catherine is leaving. Please ensure she is escorted from the house."

She inched her head higher and sniffed. "I have said my piece in any case." With a smirk, she pointed a bony forefinger at me. "You will soon see that I am correct." She traipsed from the room, followed by Slade and John. Our butler must have foreseen a possible need for the footman's assistance.

Once the front door had closed after the hateful woman's departure, I approached Slade. "Notify all the servants that Lady Catherine is not to enter this house again until further notice."

"Yes, madam."

"Thank you, Slade." I left him at a rapid walk. I broke into a run on the staircase as a tear trickled towards my cheek. I did not reduce my pace until I reached my room, where I collapsed in my armchair and indulged in an unrestrained fit of weeping for several minutes.

Despite my unwholesome curiosity for the topic, I had never questioned Fitzwilliam on the subject of Miss Comerford. Instead, I had clung to the conviction that any possible intimacy between them remained in the past. Had I been wrong?

And what sort of connexion did he have to Mrs. Fraser? Might he have fathered her dark-haired daughter? Could the former Miss Townshend have loved Fitzwilliam enough to be intimate with him and yet wed another man because of a quarrel? Since I dared not broach the matter with Mrs. Fraser, I had no way of ascertaining the truth.

Or did I? Mrs. Stapleton, a sensible soul whom I trusted, had a close association with Mrs. Townshend. Maybe she could allay my fears, at least those ascribable to Mrs. Fraser. I scrawled a message to my friend, asking her to have tea with me tomorrow. If not for my family and friends who awaited me in the dining-parlour, I might have hidden in my chamber the rest of the evening. Instead, I washed my face, collected myself, and went downstairs to rejoin the others.

CHAPTER 7
Disturbing Testimony

Thursday, 14 November
Darcy House

JANE AND I STAYED UP TALKING UNTIL TWO O'CLOCK LAST night. My dear sister's calm and consoling companionship acted as a balm to my inner turmoil. I elicited the details of Mr. Bingley's marriage proposal and the plans she and he had made. In return, I recounted my impressions of Brighton and the most notable people I had met in London. Of course, I did not burden my sister with my worries concerning Miss Comerford or Mrs. Fraser.

As an early riser, I had planned to walk in the park before my guests awoke. Once dressed, I took Rory downstairs and met John and Martin in the vestibule. "I am ready to leave."

"Very good, madam." John moved ahead to open the front door.

"Wait please, Mrs. Darcy."

I whirled towards Mr. Webb's voice.

He came towards me in the hall. "Do you intend to leave the house?"

"Yes, I shall walk in Hyde Park." I gestured to the two footmen, both built on a large scale. "John and Martin are armed—not to mention Rory will be with us."

"Nevertheless, I should like to accompany you as well if you will allow it."

"By all means."

He collected his warm garments, and we moved into the chilly morning air. As we descended the front steps, my sight riveted upon the bench across the street, and I halted—the dark-haired, bearded man had returned; this time, he read a small book. I reached for Mr. Webb's arm.

"What is the matter?"

"The man seated on the bench across the street. He was there yesterday. I think he may be watching the residence."

Mr. Webb gave the man a furtive glimpse. "Take Rory and your footmen and step back into the house. It will appear less threatening if I approach the man alone. I shall talk to him and return to you."

"Please be careful."

He nodded. "I shall."

John, Martin, Rory, and I returned to the vestibule. Too restless to sit, I paced in the hall with my dog trotting behind me. No more than ten minutes later, Mr. Webb returned, and I strode towards him.

He gave me a slight smile. "He is harmless—a reporter with *The Morning Post* who hoped to get a story. I convinced him to leave, and

I doubt he will return. Still, I suggest you instruct Slade to have your servants be watchful and notify you if they see any other suspicious people."

"Thank you, I shall do so. I suppose the man has a job to carry out, but...he need not perform it here."

"Quite right. I have no reason to doubt the man's word, but in the interest of prudence, I shall write to Mr. Ellis at the Alien Office and provide a description of him with a summary of our conversation."

"Yes, that is a good idea."

We entered Hyde Park, and I adopted my usual brisk pace. Mr. Webb gazed at me with raised eyebrows but did not comment on my gait. Few people traversed the promenade towards Kensington Gardens at this hour, but a lone figure approached us in the distance. When the man drew nearer, his well-favoured visage became distinguishable: *Lord Kentwood.* I feigned an interest in the ducks swimming in the Serpentine to my right. Since Mr. Webb accompanied me rather than my husband, the marquess would not be apt to notice—

"Mrs. Darcy!"

Darn, he recognised me. I met Lord Kentwood's gaze and returned his wave.

The marquess increased his pace until he stopped before me. "This is a fortunate circumstance. Good morning."

"Good morning, Lord Kentwood." Sharpness characterised my salutation. I should keep the encounter as brief as possible.

He stepped closer, and his mouth tugged at a frown. "I am so sorry you have been plagued with this frightful business of Darcy's disappearance. What a grievous situation for you and your family! How are you, if I may ask?"

"I am as well as may be expected." After obtaining Lord Kentwood's consent, I introduced Mr. Webb to the marquess, who responded with a brusque nod.

His lordship folded his hands and beheld me with a rumpled brow. "Ever since I heard the unfortunate news, I have been most concerned for your welfare. This is why I stopped by the house on Wednesday, so I could offer you my full support."

"I thank you. That is kind of you." His calling card had been among the stack I had received yesterday.

"It is a relief to know you have the assistance of a...friend." The marquess glanced at Mr. Webb, then at John and Martin, who stood ten feet behind us. "And you are wise to have servants with you—a lady like you cannot be too careful. There have been several instances of rogues preying upon the gentry in the park these past few months."

"Yes, I understand the need for caution."

He glanced down at Rory, who sat at my side. "You have a beautiful dog."

"Thank you."

"Since you are new to London, you may be unaware that I have a wide acquaintance and a great deal of influence in this town. Rest assured I am at your disposal for any resource or service you may require at any time."

"I appreciate that, my lord."

"Not at all. It would be my pleasure to help you. Please do not forget that."

I forced the edges of my lips upwards. "I shall remember."

"Well, I wish you a good day. I am very glad we had this talk." Lord Kentwood flashed an inviting smile, tipped his hat, and continued on his way.

We moved forwards again and resumed my desired gait.

Mr. Webb took a quick look behind us. "The marquess appeared eager to be of service to you. Are you well acquainted with him?"

"No, we met last week." I wrinkled my nose. "And my husband does not have a high opinion of the man." *To say the least.* "So, he is the last man I should ever turn to for assistance."

"I see."

Back at the house, Georgiana, Mr. Webb, and I spent a leisurely two hours at the breakfast table with my father and Jane. Papa regaled us with the recent antics of his friends and neighbours. Jane, in turn, described the progress being made by Mary, Kitty, and Lydia in their studies. All the while, I focused upon maintaining a tranquil appearance—a task made easier by my father and sister, whose presence buoyed my spirits.

At noon, Mr. Bingley arrived to convey them home to Hertfordshire. I embraced my father and sister and fought tears throughout our farewells.

Mrs. Stapleton arrived at one o'clock, and Slade took her to the morning room as I had requested. When I joined her, she came towards me and took both of my hands. "How do, my dear?"

"I am better now for seeing you. Thank you for coming."

She peered at me. "You look exhausted. What has happened since yesterday? Have you received any word of Mr. Darcy?"

"No, unfortunately not."

"Well, it is evident something has occurred. You must tell me what is weighing upon you." Mrs. Stapleton led me to the sofa.

We bided our time as two of the maids brought in refreshments. When they left, I poured tea for us. I attempted to remain impassive as I related Lady Catherine's speech from the night before. I omitted any mention of Mrs. Fraser's child, for I could not bear to repeat that dross.

Even so, Mrs. Stapleton dropped her plate of walnut biscuits on the table with a clatter. "For heaven's sake, what an odious woman! I never cared for Lady Catherine, but I should not have believed her to be capable of this much wickedness. For her to tell you this poisonous prate now, when you are anguished over your husband's disappearance, is contemptible."

She took my teacup from my hand and set it on the table. "I trust you will forgive my presumption, but I imagine you may need this." Her arms enveloped me. "You poor dear. I hope you instructed your servants not to allow that woman back into this house."

"I have done so, yet I hate being the cause of separating my husband from his late mother's only sister."

"Not at all—the fault is hers. And *you* are his first priority."

For a moment, I allowed her welcome assurance to settle over me. But the spectre of Mrs. Fraser soon urged me to speak. I brushed my fingers under my watery eyes before withdrawing to face her. "I... um...thought that, since you and Mrs. Townshend are so well acquainted, you might know whether my husband and Mrs. Fraser had ever been...in love."

"Pray, do not allow Lady Catherine's vicious words to torment you." Mrs. Stapleton rested a hand on my arm. "Mrs. Townshend never knew for certain the extent of her eldest daughter's sentiment for Mr. Darcy. I know my friend would have been delighted if the two had married, but it was not to be."

"Do you know whether Mrs. Fraser married her husband for love?"

"From my observation of the former Miss Hannah Townshend with her betrothed, Mr. Fraser, I believe she did. And I have no doubt whatsoever that Mr. Darcy loves you." Mrs. Stapleton lifted her teacup and took a sip. "Now you must promise me that you will not waste another moment fretting over Lady Catherine's twaddle."

"No, I shall not."

"That is well." Mrs. Stapleton put a small cinnamon cake on a plate and held it out for me. "Now as I recall, you are partial to these. I shall not leave until you have consumed it."

I accepted the plate. "Thank you. I believe I can manage that."

Mr. Webb and I spent an unproductive fifteen minutes with a brutish, unkempt blacksmith who reeked of alcohol. The man maintained he had observed Fitzwilliam the night before in a tavern. But he altered his story several times and could not describe the appearance of the person he purported to be my husband beyond stating the gentleman was tall and dark-haired.

I had spent half an hour at the pianoforte in the music room when Slade announced that Lord Berkeley had called for me. I took a moment to brace myself before I joined the viscount in the drawing-room. What criticism or unwanted advice would he have for me today?

But he pranced forwards to greet me with his usual arrogance subdued in favour of a more sanguine demeanour.

When we took seats, he sobered. "I take it you have had no tidings of Darcy."

"No, I am afraid not."

He shifted to the edge of the chair, and his handsome features compressed in a depiction of concern. "I have made enquiries of Darcy's friends at my club, but so far, none have borne any fruit. The situation is as puzzling as it is distressing."

"Yes, quite distressing." I glanced at the service bell. "May I offer you refreshments?"

"No, thank you." He held me in a probing gaze. "I am concerned for you. Compared with two days ago, you appear wearier and frailer."

I pressed my shoulders back. Maybe a straighter posture would convey vigour. "Nevertheless, I am well."

"You are an admirable lady." He raised a hand to his chest. "I cannot imagine what these past few days have been like for you. You must be half out of your mind with worry. Most women in your place would take to their beds. And who could blame them? After all, each day, each hour that passes with no news of Darcy's whereabouts makes it ever less likely we shall see him alive and well again."

I raised my chin. "He *shall* return—of that, I have no doubt."

"Pray, excuse me, I ought to have tempered my speech. It is natural for you to cling to hope, and far be it from me to take it away from you."

My slippered foot tapped upon the floor. Why had he come?

The viscount smoothed the fabric of his tailcoat and presented a toothy smile. "It occurs to me that, as we are now cousins, we should not be so formal. I should be pleased if you would call me Berkeley."

"Very well, Berkeley. You may call me Elizabeth."

"Yes, Elizabeth, the name suits you well." He adjusted his feet and leaned forwards. "Although Darcy is a responsible and astute man, he and I do not always agree. In particular, the more I consider the peculiar burden he has put on you, the more it bothers me. Darcy must have come to this extraordinary resolution because of his excessive fondness for you. I fancy he supposed it might amuse you to make inconsequential decisions whilst he is away from the house, but he could not have foreseen a misadventure that would detain him for days on end."

Ah, the viscount revealed his object at last: he wanted to discuss my husband's business matters.

"Furthermore, he failed to consider the delicate nature of females—those of your sex lack the mettle and stamina of males. No lady ought to be saddled with so much responsibility, not even in the best of times. And whilst you are facing this profound adversity, it is insupportable."

"I assure you I can handle the responsibility. In actuality, I welcome the endeavour, for it distracts me from other concerns. Besides, it pleases me to know I am adhering to Fitzwilliam's wishes."

His mouth twisted downwards. "Nevertheless, I know my cousin very well, and I am certain he would not want you to be overtaxed at a time when you are grieved. Therefore, I have devised a solution—a way to free you from this hardship." He reached into his coat pocket, withdrew a packet of papers, and placed it on the table between us. "To that end, I had these documents prepared for your signature."

My gaze fell upon the bundle. "What is the aim of this paperwork?"

"All you need to do is sign this, and you will transfer all financial responsibility to me. I shall handle Darcy's business concerns until he returns." He strode to the escritoire and returned with a bottle of ink and a pen, placing them before me. "This way, you will be free to devote your time to more appropriate pursuits."

"Your concern is appreciated, but I cannot accept your...help."

A vein popped up on his temple. "Do not be foolish. Of course you can and must accept my assistance—we are family after all. Sign the contract and leave these financial concerns to me. You must know that as an educated gentleman, I can take far better care of Darcy's financial interests than you could ever hope to do." He opened the packet to the second page and pointed to a signature line. "Just write your name here."

"I do not doubt you have benefited from the best possible education, but I shall not—"

"Pray do not make a hasty decision. In my capable hands, Darcy's coffers could increase at a swift pace. Allow me to provide one example. I learnt yesterday of a rare investment opportunity, one that is certain to bring in a windfall of profit. If I invest the funds from Georgiana's dowry, I may double her money in less than a year."

"That sounds like an interesting possibility, but I shall leave my sister's jointure where my husband chose to invest the money. We are assured a modest but dependable return, and I am inclined to continue with his plan."

His features contorted. “Have you no concern for your sister’s financial well-being? Will you deny her the opportunity to double her wealth? Answer me, will you not reconsider?”

“I am sorry, but I must decline your offer.”

“Is that your final answer?”

“Yes, it is.”

Lord Berkeley snatched up the papers and crumpled them in his hand. “Of all the obstinate, ignorant, maddening…” He stood and pinched the bridge of his nose, then waved his index finger at me. “You may be certain Darcy will hear of your refusal to accept my assistance.” He shoved the papers back in his pocket and stalked from the room, muttering a series of curses.

With a groan, I reclined against my chair. “Goodbye, *Berkeley.*”

Crisp footfalls sounded in the hall. I straightened my spine before Slade entered the morning room.

“Madam, a street urchin is at the door. He claims to have seen the master yesterday.”

“Thank you, Slade. Please inform Mr. Webb, then bring the lad here.”

“Yes, madam.”

Minutes later, Slade escorted the boy, a skinny but robust blond-haired child of perhaps twelve, towards me. “Mrs. Darcy, this is Luke Jones.” The lad took cautious steps, staring at the furnishings with wide eyes. He wore a dirty, weathered coat, the knees of his breeches threadbare.

When the boy's sight locked upon me, he bowed. "Ma'am."

"Luke, please sit." I pointed to a chair, and he perched on the edge of the indicated seat. I dismissed Slade, who left the room as Mr. Webb entered.

I sat across from Luke, and Mr. Webb took a position at my right. I smiled at the boy. "I understand you may have seen Mr. Darcy yesterday."

"Yes, ma'am, I did."

"Are you certain you know what Mr. Darcy looks like?" asked Mr. Webb.

"Yes, sir." Luke's fingers spruced his tousled mane. "Oft times, Mr. Angelo gives me work at 'is school of arms. I've seen Mr. Darcy there. 'E's one o' the good ones—'e always gives me a coin."

My scrutiny of the lad did not reveal any obvious signs of dishonesty; he appeared composed and mature for one so young, and employment with Mr. Angelo affirmed his trustworthiness. From the way Fitzwilliam had spoken of the fencing master, the man would not tolerate anything less than efficiency and trustworthiness in his servants. "Where and when did you see Mr. Darcy?"

"I saw 'im yesterday morning at seven o'clock. I went to see the butler at Mr. Burk's 'ome at 30 Lisle Street. 'E gives me work now and again. I was walking towards the service entrance when I saw a carriage stop in the alley. Mr. Darcy came out and went to the service door at 28 Lisle Street—Miss Comerford's 'ouse."

I gasped. *Miss Comerford.* No, it could not be true! I pressed my palms together to keep my shoulders from sinking. The boy was mistaken; he must be.

"Do you refer to Miss Frances Comerford, the actress?" Mr. Webb shot me a quick look.

Thank goodness for his initiative, because I could hardly stay upright, much less pose any further questions to the lad.

"Yes sir. Mr. Darcy entered the 'ouse, and I didn't see 'im again."

"It is still rather dark at seven. How could you be certain you saw Mr. Darcy and not another dark-haired man?"

Luke frowned. "It was light enough for me to know it was 'im. I was surprised to see 'im there. That's why I watched til 'e went into the 'ouse."

"How do you know Miss Comerford resides there?"

"Several of Mr. Burk's servants 'ave mentioned 'er. They say she's famous, and they're eager to spy 'er as much as possible."

Mr. Webb stepped closer to Luke until he towered over the lad, giving him a fierce glare. "You fabricated this story, did you not?"

"You think I'm lying?" The boy shrank back against the chair. "No, sir, I didn't."

"Of course you did. You came here to get the reward offered by Mrs. Darcy."

"No! I mean, yes, I want the reward, but I didn't lie."

"Someone put you up to this, is that right? Who told you what to say?"

"Huh?" The lad's eyes widened. "I don't know what you mean. Why would anyone do that?"

Mr. Webb blew out his breath. "I know not. Maybe someone paid you to say it as a cruel hoax."

"No, sir."

"Then why did you tell us this falsehood?"

"I told the truth."

Whilst Mr. Webb continued to interrogate Luke, I retreated into a deluge of frantic conjecture. The lad's testimony must have been either fictitious or mistaken—he saw another man who resembled Fitzwilliam. Or maybe the lad thrived on attention, and this was his way of getting it.

Mr. Webb appeared in front of me, rousing me from my reverie. "I am sorry you bore witness to that boy's prattle, Mrs. Darcy. I warned him not to repeat that fable to anyone else."

I glanced around the room, now occupied by just us two. I had not noticed Luke's departure. "It was most...unexpected."

"I urge you not to give his account a moment's thought. Luke refused to admit it, but I am certain he prevaricated. No doubt he is aware of the ridiculous rubbish being published in the newspapers. It is naught but base speculation of Darcy's whereabouts. He must have decided to exploit the situation."

Try as I might, I could not accept Mr. Webb's explanation, which did not fit my impression of Luke. No, I had to determine the truth. "I want you to tell me everything you know of my husband's dealings with Miss Comerford."

"Upon my word, I do not know anything."

"It is common knowledge that he knows her."

"He has never mentioned her to me. Even if Darcy is acquainted with the lady, Luke's statement is too absurd to be taken seriously."

"Yet he made the declaration, and I cannot overlook it. I shall go to Miss Comerford's house and ask her whether she has seen my husband."

"No, Mrs. Darcy, that would not be wise. If you went there, it would fuel the rumours."

"Nevertheless, I shall go. I must know the truth."

Mr. Webb scrubbed his hands over his face. "Allow me to go in your stead. I shall talk to her."

"Thank you, but I must hear her answer for myself."

At length, he nodded. "In that case, I shall accompany you."

"Very well. I want to be done with the matter as soon as possible." I stood and moved towards the servants' bell.

"Pray, wait a moment." Mr. Webb held his hand out. "We must ensure no one sees you enter Miss Comerford's home. We should take a hired carriage, and I advise you to choose a bonnet that obscures your face."

Thank goodness for his sagacity; I should not have considered those details. "Thank you, you are correct."

28 Lisle Street, London

I perused the stately brick facade of Miss Comerford's elegant house, featuring bow-windows, iron-work railings, and a grand set of pillars around the porch, and my steps slowed. Did I have the fortitude to confront this woman? What should I do if she confirmed my worst fears?

"Mrs. Darcy, are you well? If you have changed your mind..." Mr. Webb touched my arm.

"No, thank you." I continued onwards. No matter how sordid

the truth might be, to remain in ignorance would be worse, or so I told myself.

The butler left us in a sitting room for a short while. He returned and led us into a splendid drawing-room dressed in shades of rose and gold. Miss Comerford stood at the butler's announcement of our names. She appeared shorter than I expected, no more than an inch or two taller than me. Without the theatrical cosmetics she wore on stage, she looked far more wholesome and, *darn it*, no less beautiful.

To avoid fidgeting, I locked my arms at my sides. "I hope you will excuse the intrusion, Miss Comerford. I should not have imposed upon you if not for the peculiar circumstances."

"Please think nothing of it. I am glad to meet you, Mrs. Darcy and...um..."—Miss Comerford shuffled the two cards in her hand and glanced downwards—"Mr. Webb."

He bowed at the redhead. "It is a pleasure to meet you, Miss Comerford."

The actress nodded at him and gestured to the stylish furniture nearby. "Please sit, both of you." She retook her seat. "I was most distressed to read about Mr. Darcy's disappearance. Has he been found?"

"No, he has not." I winced as my voice cracked and sat in one of a matching pair of zebrawood chairs. Mr. Webb took the other.

Miss Comerford's mouth drew downwards. "I am sorry to hear it. I do hope he will be home soon." She folded her hands and placed them on her lap. "I admit to being puzzled why you came."

With his eyebrows slightly raised, Mr. Webb angled his head to see me. I took him to be offering to question Miss Comerford on my behalf and shook my head. I beheld her. "I have received a report, and I want you to confirm whether or not it is accurate."

Miss Comerford's emerald eyes flared. "What did you hear?"

"A witness came forward who avowed to have seen my husband enter your home yesterday morning. Is that true?"

She adjusted her coral necklace, and her lips parted. "No, of course not—the very idea is ludicrous!" Lines converged on her forehead. "I wish I could be surprised that anyone would utter such a falsehood. Because of my profession, I am often the subject of speculation and gossip. And with Mr. Darcy's disappearance and your recent marriage, there is a heightened interest in you both. Many ladies in town aspired to become Mrs. Darcy, and I imagine a fair portion of them are jealous and resentful towards you for having succeeded where they failed."

My respiration slowed to a regular rhythm. She gave every indication of earnestness. Yet how could I be certain of Miss Comerford's verity? A talented performer such as she could be convincing in a prevarication to suit her purpose. I coughed to dislodge a lump in my throat. "The person who claimed to have observed my husband yesterday was adamant of whom he had seen."

Miss Comerford's fingers traced her bottom lip. "Oh, I know what must have happened—your eye-witness saw my brother Robert. He stays with me whenever he is in town. He and Mr. Darcy have a passing resemblance, though my brother has a stockier figure."

I released a sigh. This brother must be whom Luke had seen.

We soon took our leave of the actress. Back inside the hired coach, Mr. Webb sat opposite me and tugged on his cravat, loosening the knot. "Well, I am glad Miss Comerford provided a satisfactory explanation. Now we know the lad, Luke, did not dissemble. He made an honest mistake. You may put this episode to rest."

"Yes." I directed my gaze to the houses outside the carriage window. Miss Comerford, not unlike Mrs. Fraser, presented herself well. Due to her profession, Fitzwilliam would not have considered Miss Comerford as a potential wife. However, after having met her, I could not point to any flaws of character, conduct, or appearance to assure myself that he would not have found her extremely attractive and could not have fallen in love with her.

And if he had loved her in the past, would such a powerful sentiment ever disappear completely?

CHAPTER 8

Rumours and Prophecy

Friday, 15 November
Darcy House

I ATTEMPTED TO MAINTAIN AN UNRUFFLED PRESENCE FOR Mrs. Hurst and Miss Bingley, who sat across from me in the drawing-room and gave me undisguised stares. I had no affinity for either of them, having been subjected to their airs and pettiness in Hertfordshire. Nevertheless, I overcame my disinclination to receive them for the sake of my dearest Jane; after all, they would soon be family.

Mrs. Hurst, the elder, shorter, and plumper sister, brushed her hand against her light-brown hair, arranged in an intricate pattern of plaits and ringlets. A faint sprinkling of freckles covered her ruddy complexion.

With her thick, russet mane, graceful figure, and large, hazel eyes, Miss Bingley ought to have been the more attractive of the pair, but she had an unfortunate habit of skewing her mouth and jaw in a way that conveyed scorn. She set down her teacup and twitched her aquiline nose. "My goodness, Mrs. Darcy, I am quite concerned for your health. You are so altered since the last time we met. I dare say, if we had passed each other on the street, I should not have known you."

Hyperbolic, and to my mind false, sympathy characterised Miss Bingley's manner. I had little patience for such guile. Did she even know how to be genuine? "I assure you that I am well."

"Oh, but you must take better care of yourself." Miss Bingley leaned closer to obtain a better view of me. "Your eyes have a sunken appearance, and you are so pallid and drawn. It is apparent you have lost weight." She nudged Mrs. Hurst's upper arm. "Do you not agree, Louisa?"

For goodness' sake. I did not look as bad as that. Did I?

"Why, yes." Mrs. Hurst made a show of examining me, as though for the first time. "My sister is correct—the overt deterioration in your health is most alarming."

"It is apparent that this unfortunate ordeal has prematurely aged you." Miss Bingley's expression came just short of a smirk. "You ought to be under a doctor's care. I should be happy to give you the direction of our family physician."

Of all the nerve! I crossed my ankles and took a calming breath. I did not look my best, which was natural after missing sleep and lacking an appetite, but they had no call to use such stark language and exaggerate the situation. "That will not be necessary."

"Oh, well"—Miss Bingley shared a look with her sister—"no doubt you would prefer to see Mr. Darcy's physician."

Mrs. Hurst nodded.

"We are excessively concerned for Mr. Darcy's well-being." Miss Bingley sipped her tea. "He has been a close friend of ours for years, and nothing remotely similar to this has ever occurred before. Until now, I have always considered him to be one of the most reliable and admirable gentlemen of my acquaintance."

What did she mean to imply?

"Have you had any word at all from him?"

"I have not."

"What a pity." Miss Bingley raised a palm towards me. "Now I caution you not to pay any attention to the rumours that have been spreading with regard to Mr. Darcy's whereabouts. Many people are of the opinion he has not suffered a misfortune at all. They say he has taken a mistress—either a former one like Miss Comerford or Mrs. Fraser, or a new one yet to be identified." She glanced at Mrs. Hurst. "According to my brother-in-law, it is a frequent topic of conversation at his gentlemen's club."

I stifled a gasp. Had she no shame?

"Oh, yes." Mrs. Hurst fixed upon me. "My husband mentioned that several bets are in play at White's as to the lady's identity. Is it not peculiar how men will find any excuse for a wager?"

The callous shrews! My hands curled into fists. For Jane's sake, I should refrain from striking either of them. Instead, I should remove myself from their abuse. I stood and attempted to retain a modicum of poise. "On second thoughts, I feel a fever coming on, so I urge you both to depart at once. Pray do not return until I have sent word that it is safe. I should hate to pass my illness on to either of you." I smiled at the two gawking ladies and strode from the room.

Once I had asked Slade to see them out, I proceeded to the study. An hour or so later, I glanced up from a pile of missives as footfalls in the hall grew closer. Slade appeared at the open doorway. "Madam, a Romani woman has asked to see you but would not reveal her purpose. Shall I send her away?"

"No. Please notify Mr. Webb and give us a few minutes before you bring her to the morning room. And I should like tea served as well."

Slade adopted a stiff posture; his jaw lowered.

"Is there anything else?"

He entered the room. "Excuse me, madam, but I have observed many of her kind to be criminals."

"Nevertheless, I shall receive her."

"Yes, madam." Slade departed.

On my way to the morning room, I encountered Mr. Webb. He strode towards me, his bearing stiff. "Mrs. Darcy, I caution you against meeting with this woman. I suggest you allow me to determine her object first. If she proves to have a legitimate purpose, I shall call for you."

"I see no need for that. Let us receive her together."

He released an audible breath. "As you wish."

We entered the morning room where two maids set tea and refreshments on the oblong table near a sofa and two chairs.

Slade announced Mrs. Winters, and a striking, slender woman with ebony hair and keen, dark eyes emerged from behind him. Her thick, expressive eyebrows dominated her oval countenance. I guessed her age to be forty. She wore a gown of fine sprigged muslin, and a yellow taffeta scarf had been tied around her head in an artful bow. Her gaze darted around the room, lingering for a moment on Mr. Webb before fixing upon me. "You must be Mrs. Darcy."

"Yes." I glanced to my left. "And this is Mr. Webb."

The two exchanged curt nods.

"Please, Mrs. Winters, have a seat."

She chose one of the chairs.

I sat upon the sofa and enquired of her preference, then poured her a cup of tea. When Mr. Webb declined any refreshment and remained standing, I filled a cup for myself.

She sniffed the steaming liquid and took a sip. "This isn't bad for English tea, though I much prefer my own dandelion brew." She held Mr. Webb in an intent look. "What I have to say to Mrs. Darcy is private."

Mr. Webb stepped closer to loom above her, and his eyes narrowed to slits. "I do not know what sort of scheme you have in mind—whether you hope to swindle your way to the reward money or if intimidation is more your style. Either way, I shall remain to ensure you do not take advantage of Mrs. Darcy."

"You are rude, prejudiced, and mistaken." Mrs. Winters stretched to an erect deportment. "Look at my dress, my scarf. Do I appear destitute to you? I dare say my clothes are a great deal finer than yours."

With a sharp inhalation, Mr. Webb rolled back upon his heels.

For the first time, I took notice of his coat and trousers, which fit him ill and seemed to be of mediocre quality. Did this lend credence to my uncle's far-fetched theory of him having taken the *real* Mr.

Webb's place? No, I could not believe that my guest, whom I now considered to be a friend, would deceive me.

Mr. Webb must not patronise a skilled tailor, and perhaps he did not benefit from a competent and fastidious valet like my husband did. Not all gentlemen placed a high priority upon their appearance.

"Well, madam, what say you?" Mrs. Winters viewed me with her brows pitched upwards.

I stood. "Please excuse us for a moment." I gestured to Mr. Webb. "May I have a word with you in the hall?"

"Yes, of course." Mr. Webb went ahead, held the door for me, and closed it behind him. "I suppose you think she seems harmless enough. Well, you ought to know I have dealt with Romanies many times in the past. I am aware of the trickery they often use—not just the men but women and children as well. I strongly advise against you speaking alone with that...woman."

"Your past experience notwithstanding, there is no reason to think she wishes me any harm."

"I disagree. If she had an honourable reason to come here, she would not have insisted upon meeting you alone. No doubt she expects you will be easier to bamboozle if you are without support."

"Nevertheless, I shall listen to her."

Mr. Webb gnashed his teeth. "You are a stubborn lady." He paced the length of the hall, spun round, and strode back towards me.

I held my ground and stiffened in preparation for his next argument.

However, the tension in his features abated. "You are exasperating, Mrs. Darcy, yet I cannot help but admire your determination. I shall await you here."

"You need not." I canted my head towards John, stationed nearby. "If I were to call out, he would hear me."

"Maybe so, but I shall not rest easy until the woman departs."

"Very well." I returned to the morning room and found Mrs. Winters tucking into a slice of apple cake. I resumed my seat. "Why do you want to see me?" I drank from my teacup.

"That will not be easy to explain. I have information to convey. In a manner of speaking, I have a message—from Mr. Darcy."

I choked on the tea and had to cough several times. "What do you mean? Have you seen my husband? Do you know where he is?" I dabbed at my mouth with a napkin.

"No, no, I'm sorry. I don't know where he is or what happened to him." She set her plate on the table. "Allow me to explain. I am a painter and a seamstress, but *dukkering* is my primary trade."

Dukkering? Where had I heard the term before? Oh yes: she earned money as a seer. My shoulders curved in. So, Mr. Webb had the right of it.

"I have more than two dozen clients in London alone who consult me on a regular basis. They seek my guidance when they encounter problems or momentous decisions, and they pay me well. Maybe you have heard of me: 'The Mysterious Madame Winters'."

"No, I have not been in town long. In truth, I do not believe in fortune-telling." I steeled my frame.

But rather than take offence from my statement, Mrs. Winters smiled as though amused. "I am not surprised. You are clever, sensible, and kind."

Did she hope flattery would put me off my guard? "You do not know anything about me. We never met before today."

"Yes, but I am far more observant than most people and have learnt to heed my instincts. I sense that I can trust you."

"Trust me with what?"

"The truth. Palmistry, tea-reading, and the like—much of it is nonsense." Her nose crinkled. "Most fortune-tellers are heartless frauds. They despise their *gadje* clients and seek to bleed as much money from them as possible. I am different—first, because I have a rare gift, and second, because I have met many English folk who are decent people."

"It seems you want me to believe the others are tricksters, but not you."

"I do not always tell my clients the truth. Nevertheless, my object is to help them, not take advantage of them. I provide valuable advice and ensure they are better off for knowing me."

"You may be a superior actress to others in your profession, but you are no less of a deceiver. You take money under false pretences."

Mrs. Winters shrugged. "Deception is often a necessary part of the performance. I have a keen instinct for judging people and deducing what they need, which is not always what they want. I could use my vocation for evil as many others do, but I don't."

"I am glad to hear it." Her earlier statement echoed in my ears. "You profess to have a divine message from my husband."

"Yes. From time to time, I have visions. I cannot control their nature or when they come. Earlier today, I had a vision of Mr. Darcy. This is why I came to see you."

I raised a hand to my thumping heart. How dare she taunt me this way? "Why should I believe you when you have admitted to being a liar?"

"I have not lied to *you,* and I shall not." Her lips twisted in a wry style. "I have never been this frank with a *gadje* before."

"Why would you see my husband in a vision? You do not even know him." My throat compressed. "Or do you?"

"I have never been introduced to Mr. Darcy, yet I do know him. I know he is honourable. There are few gentlemen who would step in to assist a stranger in need, especially one of my kind. But your husband did so in the spring of 1810."

Mrs. Winters settled back in her chair. "My family had a booth on Bond Street where we sold our wares—my paintings, scarves, jewellery, and other trinkets. My daughter, Selina, was fourteen then—a beautiful child with the form of a grown woman. My husband and son had gone to meet a merchant in Kent. I hesitated to leave her alone at the booth to buy bread at the bakery, but Selina insisted she would be well without me. So, I went."

She stared into her teacup and grimaced. "While I was gone, two...*gentlemen* came to the booth. They pretended to be interested in one of the paintings. The men suddenly moved to either side of Selina and grabbed her arms. One of them covered her mouth to prevent her from crying out. They pulled her towards a nearby alley. When I left the bakery, I spotted them dragging my daughter. She struggled to free herself, but they overpowered her. I yelled at the men to let her go, but I was too far away for them to hear. Several other gentlemen rushed by them, averting their eyes to the assault."

I inched forwards, tensing my spine in dread of what she might say next.

"But one gentleman rushed towards them, a handsome, dark-haired stranger. He struck the taller brute hard enough to send him stumbling to the ground. The second attacker released Selina and ran away. The dark-haired man led my terrified daughter to the chair at our booth.

"When I reached them, the assailant got to his feet. He cursed Selina's saviour and called my daughter a whore. I confronted the wretched man and took satisfaction at the sight of his bloody, mangled nose." Mrs. Winters displayed a vindictive grin. "I spat in his eyes. He raised his hand to strike me, but the dark-haired gentleman came towards us, and the fiend's arm dropped to his side. The coward backed away and fled."

"I am so sorry your daughter suffered such a harrowing incident. I hope she is well recovered now."

"Thank you, yes. And my husband has taught Selina how to defend herself in case she should ever encounter a similar situation." Mrs. Winters adjusted the silk scarf higher upon her head. "Anyhow, I offered to give the gentleman his choice of anything from our wares in thanks, but he declined. He declared he had done no more than his duty as a gentleman. After he walked away, I overheard another man greet him as 'Mr. Darcy'. I remembered the name as well as his face. So you see, I have a compelling incentive to help your husband."

I did not question the veracity of her account. Fitzwilliam would not hesitate to protect a lady in imminent danger, stranger or not. And a mother would not manufacture a story of this nature involving her daughter. "I should like to know what happened in your vision."

"It lasted no more than a minute. I had a temporary connexion to Mr. Darcy in which I felt what he felt, saw what he saw, and knew his thoughts."

What a fantastic claim! Did she expect me to believe this?

"He was frustrated, angry, and most of all anxious for your sake and for being kept from you. He pictured you at Hyde Park wearing a blue pelisse and on a beach in a green cape."

My breath hitched. Could she really have made a mental connexion with Fitzwilliam? I should not be so quick to accept her account. She could have observed me last week in my blue pelisse. Still, how would she know I had a green cape, which I had worn in Brighton and nowhere else? Of course, many ladies had green capes or cloaks—she may have made a calculated guess. Yet, what if she spoke the truth? I gripped the arms of my chair. "How did he look? Was he...injured in any way?"

"I cannot be certain, but I could see no obvious signs of injury, and he did not seem to be in pain." Mrs. Winters cocked her head. "It is apparent that you are doubtful. I can understand why you would be sceptical, but I have no reason to deceive you."

"You tell your clients whatever they wish to hear, do you not?"

"When I believe it is in their best interests, then yes."

"Are you not doing the same with me?"

"If I had intended to tell you a pretty lie, I should not have confided in you. Mr. Darcy is grieved. He longs to return to you, but he cannot, not yet."

"I have believed all along that my husband will return. He must."

"In my vision, Mr. Darcy did not doubt he would reunite with you, but he did not know when."

How confounding, and yet...encouraging, if her assertions could be relied upon.

Her mouth pressed flat. "You must be aware of the gossip

spreading around town, the unsavoury speculation on where your husband might be...and whom he may be with." She stared at me. "Ah, I see you have heard it."

Darn. I had tried to remain impassive. What betrayed me?

Mrs. Winters waved her hand. "You must not allow those rumours to distress you. You will discover soon enough that they are lies spread by ignorant and spiteful people out of malice or jealousy. Mr. Darcy has no room in his heart for any other lady. Most people don't understand the power of a great love, for they have never experienced such feelings. You, Mrs. Darcy, are cherished. The force of your husband's sentiment and his great admiration for you convinced me that I could speak plainly to you, and you would listen."

I suppressed a sob. I could not resist the temptation to believe her, at least for the moment. "Is someone holding my husband captive?"

"Alas, I don't know." Her dark eyes crinkled. "I have one additional impression to convey. This concept came to me at the conclusion of the vision and is not known to Mr. Darcy. You must warn him when you next see him. Tell him that someone he trusts will betray him and put him in danger."

That sounded like the usual sort of melodramatic fortune-teller prattle. Yet I could not completely dismiss her advice. "Can you provide any more details? Will it be a friend or a relative, a male or a female?" An image of a sneering Lord Berkeley came to mind.

She shook her head. "It could be any of those. When Mr. Darcy returns, you must tell him to be wary."

When he returns. "I shall do so."

Mrs. Winters got to her feet. "I must go now."

I stood. "Thank you for coming, Mrs. Winters."

"You're welcome, Mrs. Darcy."

When she had gone, I fell back into my seat. Mrs. Winters had raised more questions than she answered. Yet I could not be sorry for having met her.

Mr. Webb returned to the room and closed the door behind him. "I followed her to ensure she left the house." He sat in the chair Mrs. Winters had vacated. "Are you well?"

"Yes, perfectly so."

"Did she threaten you in any way?"

"No, far from it. We had a civil conversation."

"What did she tell you?"

"Well, she is a fortune-teller."

He slapped a hand on his thigh. "I knew it! I suppose you paid her to read your palm."

"No, she never suggested I show her my palm, nor did she ask for money. She...um...said that Fitzwilliam will return home, but she did not know when."

"Did she say anything else?"

"She assured me that he loves me."

He snorted. Moments later, his cheeks reddened. "Forgive me, but anyone could have told you that. You and Darcy are new-marrieds after all."

"In any case, she made no mention of my newspaper advertisement and did not want anything from me. You misjudged her."

Mr. Webb rubbed his jaw. "Maybe I did. On the other hand, this could have been the first part of her stratagem, meant to gain your confidence. I should not be surprised if she returned with a proposal to bring Darcy home—for the right price."

"We shall see."

Late that evening, Slade knocked upon my chamber door. "Forgive the disturbance, madam. A message came for you from Mr. Gardiner's home."

I set aside the book on my lap and leaped from the armchair. I cracked open the door, accepting the sealed paper. "Thank you, Slade."

"The messenger awaits your reply."

"I shall have it shortly."

Slade nodded and closed the door. I opened my uncle's note:

15 Nov, London

My dear Lizzy,

Mr. Notley has conducted his investigation. He wants to meet with you as soon as possible. He proposed we come to your residence tomorrow at 2 o'clock. Please let me know if you need to change the time; otherwise, we shall see you then.

The investigator did not reveal his findings to me, so I shall be as anxious as you are to learn what, if anything, he discovered.

With love,
Uncle Gardiner

I wrote a response providing my agreement and gave it to Slade for the messenger.

CHAPTER 9

Mr. Notley's Report

Saturday, 16 November
Darcy House

"...AND THAT'S WHEN I SAW MR. DARCY. 'E STOOD AT THE 'azard table. I know what 'e looks like because I work at the bookshop on Finsbury Square, and 'e's come in many times." Seth Johnson, a seventeen-year-old shop-boy, glanced at me before returning his attention to Mr. Webb. "I suppose 'e must 'ave been in his cups last night because I ain't never seen him so talkative afore."

The young man provided his testimony in a sincere, mindful fashion, inspiring a sinking sensation in my stomach. A moment later, though, it occurred to me whom the young man must have observed. "Seth, are you familiar with my husband's cousin, Lord Berkeley?"

The lad shook his head. "No, ma'am."

It had to have been the viscount whom Seth had seen last night. I glanced at the mantle clock; I had fifteen minutes until my meeting with my uncle and Mr. Notley. Per my instructions, Slade would bring them to the study. I raised my hand towards Mr. Webb to catch his attention and asked him for a private word. We left the room, and I related my opinion.

"I am certain you are correct. I do not believe for a moment that the lad saw Darcy last night."

"If you do not mind, I think I shall walk in the garden." I maintained a smile despite my discomfort for the deception.

"By all means. I shall conclude matters with Seth." He drew his mouth into a taut line. "You will remain within the gate, will you not?"

"Yes, I shall."

Upon leaving him, I hastened to the study. To keep busy, I organised the day's correspondence. Soon enough, Slade appeared to announce my uncle and Mr. Notley, a slim, blond man.

Uncle Gardiner came to me and took my hand. "How are you, Lizzy?" His brows knitted as he inspected me.

"I am well, Uncle." Miss Bingley's critical speech from yesterday came back to me. Did I look haggard? At any rate, my uncle resisted expressing concern for my health, maybe due to the investigator's presence.

Uncle Gardiner glanced at the blond gentleman. "Mrs. Darcy, I should like to introduce Mr. Jeremy Notley, a principal officer at the Bow Street office."

I curtsied and met the investigator's piercing blue eyes. "I am pleased to meet you, Mr. Notley."

Mr. Notley bowed. "It is an honour meeting you, Mrs. Darcy."

"Have you...found my husband?"

"Alas, no."

I frowned and shifted to view my uncle. "Since we last spoke, I have had no news from the Alien Office."

Uncle Gardiner tilted his head. "I do not suppose your newspaper advertisement has drawn anyone with helpful information."

"Not as of yet." My sight veered to the liquor decanters. "May I offer you gentlemen a drink?"

"Thank you, Lizzy," said my uncle. "I should prefer brandy."

"Yes, I should like the same." Mr. Notley held my gaze. "And I suggest you have a small one as well."

Did he imagine his report would shock me? A tremor impaired my legs on the way to the cabinet, but I continued and poured the drinks. I had tried brandy but once, a couple of years ago in Papa's study, and disliked the taste at the time. Still, I took Mr. Notley's advice so I should have the liquor at hand. Uncle Gardiner came to pick up his and the investigator's drinks. We sat near the fireplace.

With one long gulp, Mr. Notley almost emptied his glass. "I have a prior acquaintance with Mr. Ellis. The Alien Office often seeks our assistance, and we have referred criminal matters to them on occasion. However, in my experience, the information tends to flow in one direction. It is rare for an Alien Office investigator to reveal any more details than they must. I met with Mr. Ellis on Wednesday and did not learn anything beyond what he had already told you."

How frustrating—Mr. Notley had no better luck wresting information from Mr. Ellis than did Mr. Webb. "Do you consider Mr. Ellis and his colleagues to be proficient investigators?"

"Yes, I have found them to be intelligent and effective."

"Did Mr. Ellis request your help with the investigation?"

"No." Mr. Notley exhibited a sardonic smile. "Nevertheless, I believe I provided him with helpful information pertaining to Evan Leeson. I had encountered the man in a prior investigation."

"Who is Evan Leeson?" My uncle's eyes narrowed. "The name sounds familiar, but I cannot place it."

"He is one of the two men who were found dead at the house in Camberwell." Mr. Notley removed a small notebook from his pocket and opened it. "Evan Leeson often worked with his brother, Eli. I stopped at Eli Leeson's lodging. According to his landlady, he had not been home since Monday. I suggested to Mr. Ellis that they make it a priority to find him, and I expect he will act on my advice."

I perked to a rigid position. "Do you think this man, Eli Leeson, may know where my husband is?"

"It is possible."

"Will you search for him as well so he might be found sooner?"

"I have already made inquiries at several places he is known to frequent with no luck. I expect the Alien Office will have more success. They have far more resources at their disposal than the Bow Street Office."

"I see." I lifted my glass and sampled the brandy. A strong, but smooth and not unpleasant, flavour coated my mouth and tongue. Either my tastes had matured or Fitzwilliam purchased a superior variety of brandy than did my father.

The investigator glanced at the door. "Do you know where Mr. Webb is at this moment?"

"I left him in the morning room not long ago. Why do you ask?"

"The man you know as Mr. Joshua Webb is a fraud. I have been unable to confirm his identity, but the information he provided is false. There is no estate in or near Southampton owned by anyone named Webb."

Mr. Webb is an imposter! I froze. How could this be? What did he hope to achieve? His conduct had been above reproach; he had acted as a true friend, and Fitzwilliam had told me to expect him!

"For goodness' sake!" Uncle Gardiner's voice rose to an intemperate volume, and his fist pounded the arm of his chair. "Why did you not warn me of this yesterday? You allowed that man to spend another night in this house, and my niece could have been harmed by him!"

"Although I had my suspicions, I did not receive confirmation of the facts until earlier today, when my associate returned from Southampton."

A lump formed in my throat. "What about the note I found? Do you know if Mr. Vane is the man's true name?"

"I do not believe so. At least, I could not confirm his name is Vane or anything else. I went to the address you wrote down, 40 Woburn Place. It is an office building rented to a business called Gordian Enterprises. No one appears to be using the property, and I could not find any evidence that the company exists."

"But there must be a Mr. Webb—my husband anticipated his arrival."

"Did Mr. Darcy mention where Mr. Webb resided?"

"No, he described him as a friend from university. Maybe the real Joshua Webb lives elsewhere, but he must exist." I folded my arms. "What could be the man's purpose in pretending to be Mr. Webb?"

"There is one way to find out." Mr. Notley slipped the notebook into his pocket. "I suggest we confront him at once."

Uncle Gardiner nodded. "Yes, let us see what he has to say for himself."

I summoned Slade to the study and told him to request Mr. Webb join me right away.

Slade made a visual sweep of the room. "Excuse me, madam, but has he not already been here?"

"No, why do you ask?"

"Mr. Webb enquired where he could find you not ten minutes ago. I directed him to the study. I understood him to be on his way here."

I moved past Slade to the doorway and called out to John, stationed at the end of the hall.

He strode towards me. "Yes, madam?"

"When did you last see Mr. Webb?"

"A few minutes ago. 'E went to the study door and raised 'is 'and as though to knock, but I guess 'e changed 'is mind. Then 'e walked away and turned towards the stairs."

My mouth fell open. Oh no! Mr. Webb must have overheard my uncle. What would he do now? I collected myself and nodded at my footman. "Thank you, John. That is all."

Mr. Notley came towards me. "Did Mr. Webb know your uncle had hired me?"

"No, he could not have known. Shall we go to his room now?"

"Yes, let us do that."

I led the way to 'Mr. Webb's' guest room. Before I reached the door, Mr. Notley held his hand out to stay me.

"Mr. Gardiner and I shall go in first."

My uncle rushed ahead of me. "Indeed, Lizzy, stay well behind us."

"Yes, I shall."

Mr. Notley opened the door, and I followed him and my uncle inside. The closet door stood open, the trunk and several drawers had been emptied and left open or ajar—the pseudo Mr. Webb had come and gone. I pointed to the few items of clothing remaining in the closet. "He departed in a hurry and left these behind."

"It is my fault he fled." Uncle Gardiner stared at the floor. "He must have heard my outburst in the study. If I had kept my temper and not raised my voice..."

"No, you are not to blame." I spoke in a soft tone. "You responded out of concern for me, which is natural. Besides, had you not hired Mr. Notley, I should still be ignorant of the truth."

My uncle's gaze lifted to me. "That is good of you to say."

I turned to the investigator. "This is all so confusing. Mr. Webb, or whoever he is, has been helpful to me. Have you any idea what he may have hoped to gain from this deception?"

"No, I am afraid not." Mr. Notley searched through the escritoire. "For this chicanery to work, he must have counted on Mr. Darcy being absent."

I swallowed. "Do you suspect he could be working with whoever is holding my husband?"

The investigator gave me a grim look. "Yes, it is a possibility."

I marched towards the window, then whirled to face Mr. Notley. "Mr. Ellis needs to be informed that the man who called himself Mr. Webb is an impostor."

"He ought to know by now. I sent a note to Mr. Ellis informing him of this fact and the other relevant details of my investigation. I expect he or another Alien Office investigator will arrive soon."

I blew out my breath. "I am glad to hear it. Thank you for all you have done."

"You are more than welcome, Mrs. Darcy. Please instruct your servants to arrest the man known as Mr. Webb if he should return—have them confine him until the Alien Office takes him into custody. I have exhausted every avenue of investigation for now. However, if you want my help in the future, you may reach me at the Bow Street Office."

"Very well. I appreciate that."

Mr. Notley took his leave of us. My uncle's fingers dug in to his temple. "Lizzy, I am inclined to send a couple of my servants here to provide you added protection for a few days at least. It would not hurt for you to have two more watchful guardians in the house."

"Thank you, but it is not necessary. Our servants are loyal and competent, and several of them are armed."

"If you are certain..."

"I am. I believe Fitzwilliam is even more exacting in his expectations of his servants than you are."

"Very well."

I sent for Slade again and imparted my instructions with regard to the man who called himself Mr. Webb. After my uncle departed, I followed the sounds of a familiar sonatina by Herr Beethoven to the music room. At my entry, Rory, who lay prone upon a plush rug, raised his head and wagged his tail. I went to him and crouched to stroke his back.

Georgiana's performance lacked its customary esprit. She even fumbled the notes several times—an unusual occurrence for her. My poor sister's suffering, like my own, increased with each successive day of Fitzwilliam's absence. When she finished the piece, I stood and clapped.

"Oh!" My sister left her seat and ambled to me. "Elizabeth, has anything happened?"

"I…um…" I pointed to the sofa. "Do you mind if we sit here for a while?"

"Of course not."

We settled on the sofa, and Rory claimed the narrow space between us on the floor. I told Georgiana everything I had learnt concerning 'Mr. Webb', from my first suspicion of him and my uncle hiring Mr. Notley to the information provided by the investigator.

She hugged herself. "I can scarcely believe this. I liked Mr. Webb. I trusted him! I felt reassured—that we had a friend watching over us."

"I felt the same way. It is difficult to accept he lied to us, but his abrupt departure leaves me no room to doubt Mr. Notley's findings."

"Thank goodness your uncle hired that investigator. Maybe now, with this new information, the Alien Office will find Fitzwilliam soon."

"I hope so."

Georgiana's lids lowered. "I have been thinking, and the only explanation that makes sense for Fitzwilliam to be gone this long without a word is that he must have suffered an injury—a serious one."

I took her hand. "You may be correct, but there is no use speculating on it. I am certain he will be home soon in any case."

My sister presented an unconvincing smile. "Yes, I am sure you are right."

I flinched at the knock upon the door.

Slade took a step inside the music room. "Excuse me, madam, Mr. Ellis has called for you."

"Please bring him here."

"Yes, madam."

Georgiana squeezed my hand. "Maybe they have found Fitzwilliam!"

"Perhaps so." I should not spoil her hopes by telling her the investigator had come in response to Mr. Notley's message. We stood at Mr. Ellis's entrance. I took in the officer's impassive aspect as we exchanged greetings. "Have you any tidings of my husband?"

"Not yet, Mrs. Darcy. I understand from your butler that the man who called himself Mr. Webb has fled the house."

"That is correct. I presume you will search for him. Maybe he will lead you to my husband."

"Rest assured we shall find him."

I introduced Mr. Ellis to Georgiana.

My sister rose from her curtsey and inspected the officer. "Have you made any progress at all in your investigation?"

"I have not been authorised to tell either of you anything at this time. I have come to ask Mrs. Darcy to accompany me to our office."

"Very well." I released Georgiana's arm.

"I shall go too." My sister stepped closer to me.

The portly investigator adjusted the cuff of his sleeve. "I am afraid that is not possible, Miss Darcy. I apologise, but my instructions are to bring Mrs. Darcy and no one else. Our offices are strictly regulated, and all visitors must have prior approval."

Georgiana took my arm again. "Excuse me, Mr. Ellis. May I have a word with my sister in private?"

"Yes, of course. I shall wait in the hall." Mr. Ellis left the music room.

My sister gripped both of my hands. "Please do not go." She used a low, forceful tone. "We were fooled by the man pretending to be Mr. Webb. How do we know whether we can trust Mr. Ellis? What if he is a fraud and intends to hurt you or take you captive? I could not bear to lose you too!" Tears clouded her blue irises.

"Please, do not fret, dearest. I am certain Mr. Ellis is authentic. Nevertheless, I shall take my pistol. Thanks to your brother, I know how to use it. I shall be safe." My sister's features remained pinched, so I scrambled for another way to pacify her. "As a further precaution, once I leave the room, call for Slade. Tell him to order one of the grooms to follow us on horseback at a discreet distance. That way, you will know where I am. I shall dawdle whilst preparing to leave so the groom has time to saddle a horse."

She nodded. "Yes, I shall do that. Please be careful."

I held her in a brief hug. "I promise to return."

During the carriage ride, I worried my lip. What could be important enough for them to bring me to the Alien Office? If they had good news, would they not have conveyed it at once? Maybe if I pressed Mr. Ellis, he would reveal a hint of what lay ahead.

When I asked, Mr. Ellis confirmed he had received the message from Mr. Notley. However, despite my best efforts, he would provide no other details. I resolved to follow my earlier advice to Georgiana and not speculate on what news might be shared once I reached the Alien Office. Instead, I paid attention to our route. Although Mr. Notley had affirmed Mr. Ellis's competency, it would not hurt to be cautious and alert; I should be forewarned if the vehicle took a suspicious course. When the carriage turned into a new street, I moved to the window and glimpsed Joe, one of our grooms, thirty yards or so behind us. Although I had meant to placate *my sister* with this measure, I breathed easier and relaxed against the squabs.

The driver stopped before a large office building on Crown Street. Mr. Ellis ushered me into the structure and bade me to wait in a lobby area with a table and chairs. He opened a locked door and entered a corridor, leaving me alone. After twenty minutes, the door opened again. Mr. Ellis popped his head into the room and waved to me. "Please come this way, Mrs. Darcy." We trod through a maze of passages and passed by numerous closed doors without encountering any other people.

Had all the other investigators and clerks gone home for the day? It seemed we had already walked a long way. "Where are we going?"

"It will not be much farther." Mr. Ellis halted before a door and unlocked it. He paused with his hand on the latch. "This is where we part company. You are to proceed on your own from here."

I gaped at him. What? Why would that be?

"Walk through this room and continue on past the door at the opposite end."

"Will you not tell me what to expect?"

He smiled. "I promise you there is no reason for concern."

"Very well." I held my reticule, made heavier with the reassuring bulk of my firearm, against my abdomen and entered the room, which contained naught but a desk and two chairs. Mr. Ellis closed the door after me, and the click that followed indicated he had locked me in. I tarried before the door at the other end of the room and tested it, finding it unlocked. I opened the door and crossed the threshold.

I stilled and the air escaped my lungs. *Fitzwilliam* stood from a chair situated across the room. My reticule dropped to the floor with a clang. Did my senses deceive me? Perhaps I had gone mad.

"Elizabeth." He rushed towards me.

His familiar baritone impelled me to reel forwards on quivering legs. I released a strangled sob as he took me in his arms, and I clutched him with all my strength. A frenetic dread badgered me that I must have drifted into a tantalising reverie, and if I let go of him, he would vanish. Yet the beloved scent that enveloped me and the familiar muscular form that supported me assured his actuality.

"My love, I cannot express how overjoyed I am to see you. I missed you so much!" He buried his face in my neck.

"I missed you too! We have all been frantic with worry. It has been terrible not knowing what had befallen you or if you were well. I did not know what to do, and I had to..." All at once, like an ominous cloud, the incongruity of his being there—presentable, collected, and unscathed—absorbed me, disrupting my peace.

And in the next moment, his alluring warmth transformed to a suffocating heat. I wrenched out of his arms and lurched back, scrutinising him. "I do not understand. You are not...at least you do not appear to be ill or injured. Where have you been, and why did you not contact me these past five days? For God's sake, I did not know whether you were alive or dead!"

His shoulders rounded. "I know, and I am so sorry. I—"

"*Sorry?* Do you have any notion of what I have endured or how difficult it was for me to carry on each day, remain strong for Georgiana's sake, and receive your friends with composure?"

"Elizabeth." His hand extended towards me.

I slapped it away. "Do not dare touch me!"

He held his palms up. "You have every right to be angry. And yes, I *can* imagine what you must have gone through."

"Can you?" I paced the room. "Do you have any concept of how I dreaded each night without you? Or how each successive day with no word from you added to the crushing weight upon my chest? Do you know how often I prayed for your safe return? I heard testimony from a dozen people who claimed to have caught sight of you. I endured thinly veiled insults and base innuendos from Miss Bingley and Mrs. Hurst as well as brazen contempt and vile assumptions from Lady Catherine."

His nostrils flared. "We need never see Bingley's sisters again unless you choose to. I have tolerated them thus far for Bingley's sake. What did my aunt say?"

"Among other things, she believes you fathered Mrs. Fraser's daughter."

"That is ridiculous!" A red hue overspread his complexion. "I hope you did not believe her."

"I did not know what to think. Lady Catherine alleged the child's birth occurred within seven months of Mrs. Fraser's marriage and the girl has black hair, unlike her mother and Mr. Fraser."

"Of all the despicable..." He murmured an imprecation. "I am so sorry my aunt put you through this. It is unpardonable of her to tell you such an odious lie."

"According to Lady Catherine, the girl resembles you."

He groaned. "I swore I would never reveal this, but I trust your discretion. The girl's father is Lord Kentwood. The libertine took advantage of Miss Barbara Townshend the year she turned seventeen."

I halted and folded my arms. Miss *Barbara* Townshend—the younger, more reserved sister. "How did he manage it? Did her family not take steps to protect her?"

"The Townshends had hired a companion for Miss Townshend, but the degenerate came upon her whilst she rode her horse alone at her estate. He convinced her to meet him in secret. Over a two-week period, he wooed her and professed his intention of marrying her. Once the reprobate got what he wanted from Miss Barbara, he ceased any pretence of courting her. The next time they met in a public setting, he treated her as a distant acquaintance."

"What a wretched man! I take it Mr. Townshend did not demand that Lord Kentwood marry his daughter."

"No. After the marquess's cruel rejection, Miss Townshend begged her father not to seek a marriage between them. Thus, the Townshends concealed the pregnancy. Mr. Townshend sent his daughter to have the baby at the home of a cousin in Somersetshire."

"Lord Kentwood deserves the cut direct after what he has done. Why have you not dropped the acquaintance?"

Fitzwilliam gritted his teeth. "The Townshends decided that, in order to protect Miss Townshend's reputation, they would refrain from any overt animosity towards the marquess, though they avoid him as much as possible. At their urging, I have done the same."

"It is one of our society's worst failings that a woman who is wronged by a man, whether he forced himself on her or deceived her, cannot obtain justice against her abuser without sacrificing her reputation."

"I share your frustration."

"You may be assured I shall keep the Townshends' secret."

"I know."

"The former Miss Hannah Townshend must have convinced her betrothed to claim Miss Barbara's child as his own."

"Yes."

"Mr. Fraser made a remarkable concession to his intended. He must have loved her very much."

"Without a doubt. Thus, soon after her wedding, Mrs. Fraser feigned a pregnancy. Mr. Townshend asked me to take the baby and wet-nurse to the Frasers in Scotland. I made the trip in the guise of inspecting my property there. When I arrived, Mr. Fraser gave me a tepid greeting and informed me that his wife suffered a fever. It was clear he did not welcome me there, so once the baby and nurse had settled in, I left."

"Mr. Fraser must have been jealous of you."

"If so, he had no reason to be. Maybe we simply disliked each other. I had always thought him to be brusque and arrogant."

"Did you suspect him of mistreating his wife?"

"I had no reason to believe so, and the Townshends approved of him. But I *had* wanted to see for myself that Mrs. Fraser was content in Scotland. However, I never got the opportunity." He took a hesitant step towards me. "I should never have put you through any of this if I had a choice. But now I can tell you everything that happened, and going forwards, I do not want any secrets between us."

No secrets? An image of Miss Comerford thrust to the forefront of my mind, and I swallowed. "Then I may ask you anything?"

"Yes, of course."

"In the past five days, have you been to Miss Comerford's home?"

His jaw jutted forwards. "I...um..."

"Dear Lord, you *were* with her!" I spun away from him, and my carriage shrank. Miss Comerford had lied. Had he been in her house when I called?

He moved before me. "Elizabeth, please, it is not what you might think."

What other interpretation could there be? My every muscle tensed, and my fingers clenched into fists. If he dared to touch me now, I should pound his handsome face! But as the seconds ticked by, the grasp upon my anger dwindled until I descended into despair. The actress was beautiful, a celebrated, glamorous performer, and I could not compete with her. Tears obfuscated my vision, and the floor shifted beneath me. My weight swayed from one foot to the other.

"I went there for one reason—I needed her help so I could go near our house. I hoped to obtain a glimpse of you."

"That does not make sense." My words croaked out in a whisper.

"It will, once I have explained everything. But please, you ought to sit." He gestured to a chair.

Despite my inclination to resist any suggestion of his, my legs had begun to shake again, so I took careful steps to the chair and collapsed upon it. How did Mrs. Winters fit in with all this? Maybe she knew Fitzwilliam far better than she had let on. "Did you send the Romani lady to the house yesterday?"

"Who?"

"Mrs. Winters, the fortune-teller."

"You met with a fortune-teller?"

I shook my head. "Never mind, it is not important."

"I think it is best if I begin with my association with the Alien Office." He moved another chair across from me and sat. "Three years ago, my cousin Colonel Fitzwilliam asked me to assist a friend of his—Mr. Ellis. At the time, Ellis sought a member of the *ton* to work with him in secret. I agreed, and I ended up assisting the Alien Office in several separate investigations over the space of two years."

"So, you were a...spy?"

"Yes. When I met Miss Comerford, she had already been helping the Alien Office for several years. I often associated with her at parties during that period of time whilst we worked on the same or related assignments."

"I see." My chest muscles tightened. "And whilst you colluded together, the two of you became friends and...lovers."

"*No*. We have been friends, yes, but never anything more. I swear it."

I studied his mien. "You are the picture of sincerity, but now I know you are a practised liar."

He winced. "As much as I despise duplicity, I have employed artifice at times in service to my country. But that is in the past. Now, I am free to tell you the truth. I shall never lie to you again."

"Never again? But how many times have you deceived me already? I do not even know who you are. Maybe...maybe I fell in love with a character you created, a...a phantom."

"*No!* Pray do not say that." His voice grew husky. "I am your husband, and I love you with my entire being. You are everything to me. I have always been my true self with you, and I have been as honest as possible—in every way that truly matters."

I braced my elbow upon the edge of the chair. I wanted, needed, to believe him. But should I be a fool to accept the word of a spy?

"Almost a year ago, I resigned from my work with the Alien Office. I believed that part of my life to be over. In August, Mr. Russell, an officer with the Alien Office, called on me in Ramsgate. You saw me with him that morning."

"Yes, I remember."

"He asked me to assist him with his current investigation. He complained that the man they had assigned to help him was incompetent. I refused. Then last Monday, he came to the house to inform me that another officer, Mr. Wycliff, had betrayed his oath, putting me and many others in peril."

"Why would an officer with the Alien Office do that?"

"Mr. Wycliff had been a successful investigator, and he had anticipated being promoted to the top position—superintendent. But many of his colleagues disapproved of his methods, which at times had been brutal. When Mr. Reeves received the appointment to superintendent a few months ago, Mr. Wycliff became enraged, and his behaviour grew even more erratic. Two weeks ago, Mr. Wycliff's valet reported that his master intended to sell the names of current and past spies to anyone willing to pay for them. A team of officers went to arrest Mr. Wycliff. He tried to evade them. When cornered, he drew his pistol, and they shot and killed him. Unfortunately, although they conducted a thorough search of Mr. Wycliff's house, they could not determine to whom he may have revealed the names."

I shuffled my feet. "Why did you go to the house in Camberwell?"

"The Alien Office called all current and former unofficial agents like me to an emergency meeting there—Mr Russell came to the house on Monday to ensure I should attend. I refused to go unless the office provided protection to you and Georgiana. I specified Mr. Dennis, who is one of their finest investigators, to act as bodyguard for the two of you. Mr. Russell felt certain my request would be approved. He suggested I tell you to expect a friend who would stay at the house since he anticipated we should not return until late that evening. I told you to expect Mr. Webb because it is one of Dennis's aliases. I needed to ensure you would allow him to stay."

"So the man I knew as Mr. Webb is actually Mr. Dennis."

"Yes. When I left with Mr. Russell, we stopped at the Alien Office. Once I had the superintendent's agreement to send Dennis to the house, we proceeded to Camberwell."

"My uncle Gardiner hired a Bow Street Runner, Mr. Notley. He discovered that 'Mr. Webb' did not own an estate in Southampton as he had asserted. Before we could confront him, he fled the house."

Fitzwilliam nodded. "Dennis returned to the office today to report his alias had been exposed. He is not, in fact, a member of the gentry. He is the son of a baker."

"I do not understand the need for the subterfuge. Why did you allow me to believe you were missing and possibly injured for all this time?"

He grimaced. "Without the superintendent's agreement, I could not reveal anything related to my former investigative work to you or anyone else. If I had done so, I risked being charged with treason."

"That is outrageous! I am your wife—I have every right to know the truth!"

"I know, and I am sorry. I hated lying to you, but I had no choice in the matter."

"Why are you able to tell me this now?"

"This afternoon, Mr. Reeves granted me permission to confide in you, in part because the primary focus of the investigation has been resolved, but Dennis's testimony that you are intelligent, competent, and principled persuaded him that you are worthy of trust."

"*His* testimony? Why did *you* not convince the superintendent of that?"

"I argued the point with him until he grew angry with me, but he refused to accept my word alone. He did not believe I could be objective with regard to you. No doubt he is correct."

"What happened at the house in Camberwell?"

"Ten or so of us, including Miss Comerford, had gathered there. Mr. Russell took charge of the meeting and explained what had occurred at Mr. Wycliff's residence. He instructed us to remain in our homes until the Alien Office could determine whether our association with the office had been exposed to anyone. A discussion ensued in which several people objected to being confined to their houses, when two armed men burst through the door. The first one fired his pistol, hitting Mr. Russell, who sat beside me. Many of us were armed and drew our weapons. The shooter, Evan Leeson, sustained multiple gunshots and fell to the ground within seconds. The second assailant, Eli Leeson, dropped his pistol and gave himself up. Unfortunately, neither Mr. Russell nor Evan Leeson survived their injuries."

I shuddered. "Mr. Russell sat beside you, so you could have been shot."

Fitzwilliam nodded. "Eli Leeson admitted he had been hired to kill me. He had enlisted his brother, Evan, to assist him."

"What happened to you after that? Where have you been?"

"For the most part, I have been here."

"You were never missing at all!" My hand rose to my raging heart. "Mr. Ellis lied to me and so did Mr. Webb, or rather Mr. Dennis. I still cannot believe you allowed this to happen. You could have tried harder to convince the superintendent to be reasonable. You put me and your family through days of needless anguish!"

He raked his hands through his hair. "My first object has been to ensure your safety, and I did not know whether returning home might put you in danger."

"Why should that be?" My stomach tensed. "Did you suspect the killer might make another attempt on your life?"

"Yes. Although they had Eli Leeson in custody, he did not know who had hired him. He had received an anonymous package at his home with fifty pounds and a promise of four hundred more if he succeeded in killing me. In that event, the note instructed him to appear at a particular bench in Hyde Park in three weeks' time to receive the balance of his payment. He and his brother, Evan, had planned to split the money. They followed me when I left with Mr. Russell. When they entered the house in Camberwell, they had no idea they had walked into a den of armed spies and investigators."

I pressed my palm to my head, my mind reeling from his revelations. "What happened next?"

"We all left the house and went to the Alien Office. Mr. Reeves ordered me to stay hidden until they determined who had hired the killer. He maintained my family would be safer if the suspect believed the hired assassin may have succeeded. I contended that I could take steps to ensure my family was well-protected, but he refused to allow me to leave or contact you. He believed my reappearance could compromise his investigation."

"Did they keep you in this room?"

"No, the superintendent ordered me to remain in a holding cell below stairs—a prison of sorts. Ellis took pity on me and intervened on my behalf. He devised a plan that Mr. Reeves approved—he allowed me to take the place of one of the men he had watching our house for a few hours each day if I wore a disguise and promised not to approach you or anyone in the household."

"Why was our house being watched?"

"Mr. Reeves provided the service as an additional measure of safety for you and Georgiana. They took me to Miss Comerford's home because she is a master with cosmetics and can alter a person's appearance so they are unrecognisable."

"Why did you need to go to her house? She could have come here."

"In fact, she had offered to do so and would have worn one of her disguises. But Mr. Reeves did not want her to risk leaving her house until they had identified who had hired the assassin, for they did not know who else might be in danger. They took me to her home in the early hours of the morning."

The lad, Luke, had been right after all. "I saw you across the street when Mr. Bingley, my father, and Jane arrived. You sat on the bench with the newspaper. And you returned the following day, but I never recognised you."

"You cannot know how much I longed to approach you and reassure you, but I could not. And when Dennis told me that I had made you suspicious, I had no choice but to return and remain here."

I collapsed against the chair. He had been so close to me; if only I had known! Then a new concern impelled me to perk upright. "Who hired the assassin and why?"

"Ernest Haddington, Cecil Haddington's uncle."

"The former colonel. How do they know he is responsible?"

"The Alien Office interviewed family members of those indicted in the cases in which I had participated, including Mr. Cecil Haddington. Based in part upon Haddington's account of his uncle's behaviour, the former colonel became the primary suspect."

"Why did he want to harm you?"

"He must have learnt from Mr. Wycliff that I had identified Lord Carswell as a traitor."

"*You* did that?"

He sighed. "Yes, I was disheartened to discover the truth. That case influenced my decision to end my association with the Alien Office. I suppose Ernest Haddington blamed me for the loss of his military career."

"The former colonel ought to have blamed his brother, Lord

Carswell. Why would a respected man like him, a peer, betray his country?"

"He had undertaken a series of bad investments and stood to lose his family estate, so he made a foolish, desperate decision. After his arrest, his son, Cecil Haddington, had no choice but to sell the property. And Lord Carswell's suicide left young Haddington bereft with his reputation in tatters."

"So, Ernest Haddington hired the assassin for revenge?"

"Yes. Eli Leeson received the anonymous package one day after Ernest Haddington's release from gaol. According to Cecil Haddington, his uncle had left on Tuesday without notice or any hint of his destination. This morning, Cecil Haddington informed the Alien Office of an enigmatic message his uncle had sent him from a small cottage owned by a cousin in Greenwich. The note seemed to be an adieu. A group of officers went there today. Ernest Haddington had shot himself and left a written confession."

"Does this mean you—we—are no longer in danger?"

"Yes, it is over."

Thank heavens. "What will you do now?"

Fitzwilliam rose from his chair and knelt before me. "That depends on you." His hand extended towards me but withdrew, falling to his side. "I very much want to go home...if you will allow it."

"But the house belongs to you. I cannot prevent your return."

He shook his head. "It is no more mine than yours. If you cannot forgive me...yet, if you need more time, I shall stay away." Emotion strained his baritone.

"How would you explain your absence to friends and family?"

"I should make an excuse for a sudden trip to Pemberley. The Alien Office has devised an explanation for where I have been up to now, which will be printed in the newspapers tomorrow morning."

"What account will they provide?"

"That two men attacked me, knocking me unconscious. The abductors took me to a remote cottage on the outskirts of town and held me prisoner. They sent you a ransom note, and you sought the Alien Office's assistance. They managed to recover me today, but the unknown culprits escaped."

"I understand the need for a plausible explanation for your disappearance. Still, are you not weary of having to tell falsehoods?"

"Yes, more than I can say. Yet I shall do whatever is necessary to suit your wishes."

I met his troubled, dark irises. He had offered me time—more torturous time apart—if I wanted it. But I should sooner choose death: the days without him had been a meagre form of existence. "I want...I want you to come home."

His chest heaved. "Thank you." His glistening eyes held mine, but he did not move. He awaited my cue.

I fell forwards upon my knees and slipped my arms around his waist.

He clasped me against him and rested his head on my shoulder. "Elizabeth, I love you so much!"

"You will never leave me again."

"Never." We stayed in that attitude for several minutes. Then Fitzwilliam helped me to my feet and lifted me into his arms. He carried me to an adjoining room equipped with a bed and halted beside it. His irises burned into mine. "Do I presume too much?"

Far from it—every inch of me ached for his touch. I panted next to his ear. “No.”

His mouth seized mine, and I kissed him back with all the hunger I had harnessed over the past week. He lowered me to the bed and lay beside me.

He caressed my cheek and placed delectable kisses along my chin, neck, and throat that left tingling sensations in their wake, rousing my pulse to a humming pitch. I fumbled with the buttons on his waistcoat until he laughed and undid them himself. He proceeded to remove the rest of his clothing and help me out of mine.

Our bodies united in a familiar, yet thrilling, rhythm. There, within my beloved husband’s arms, joy exhilarated my heart, and the fear and misery of the past five days faded to a distant memory.

CHAPTER 10
A Homecoming

Alien Office, Crown Street, London

I EXTRICATED MYSELF FAR ENOUGH FROM FITZWILLIAM'S embrace to lock eyes with him. "Will you take me home now?"

"By all means."

We assisted each other in dressing, but the room lacked a mirror. I posed before him, showing different views of myself. "Am I presentable?"

"Well..." He captured a lock of my hair hanging at a precarious angle and pinned it anew. "That is better." He lifted my hand and kissed my inner wrist. "You are beautiful. Although..."—his lips pursed—"you are thinner."

The dear man did not mention the shadows beneath my eyes. "My appetite has returned."

"Thank goodness for that." He retained my hand and led me back to the passage.

After we made our third turn, I beheld him. "Are you certain you can lead us out of here?"

"I have been lost in this labyrinth once or twice, but I have since learnt my way around the place." In the next corridor, a blond-haired gentleman came from the opposite direction. His step faltered upon seeing us before he continued on. Not until he came within a few yards did his features become familiar. We halted before him.

"Mr. Webb, or rather...um..." What was that name Fitzwilliam told me?

He bowed. "My name is Mr. Dennis, and I owe you an apology, Mrs. Darcy. I am sorry for the deception."

I held out my free hand. "I am pleased to make your acquaintance, Mr. Dennis, and I understand why you used an alias. My sister and I felt safer whilst you stayed with us."

He gave my hand a firm shake. "It has been my honour to be of service, Mrs. Darcy." His sight veered to Fitzwilliam. "You are a fortunate man, Darcy."

"Yes, I am." My husband shook Mr. Dennis's hand. "I appreciate everything you have done."

Mr. Dennis nodded. "A coach is waiting to take you home."

We parted from Mr. Dennis and left the building. Once inside the vehicle, I snuggled next to Fitzwilliam, and his arm wrapped around my shoulder. "Mr. Webb, or rather Dennis, had worn a wig of brown hair. I suppose he did not want anyone to recognise him."

"Yes, although he is not known to most of the gentry, he anticipated he might encounter my uncle and cousin, among others. He disguised his appearance as a precaution."

I provided Fitzwilliam a succinct summary of the correspondence I had answered in his absence and recounted the conversation I had on Thursday with Berkeley. He remained quiet, and his chin dipped. I peered at him. "What is troubling you? I know you would not want me to hand over control to your cousin."

"No, I should not trust Berkeley with any financial matter, but he made one correct point—I placed an unfair burden upon your shoulders."

"Not at all. In my view, you paid me the highest of compliments. At first, I doubted my ability to carry on in your stead. I feared your confidence in me had been misplaced. Once I became immersed in the activity, though, it provided a welcome distraction from...other concerns."

He cocked his head, studying me. "You are not just saying this to alleviate a portion of my guilt?"

"No. I am honoured you gave me the autonomy to make decisions in your absence. Most husbands never put this much trust in their wives."

"Well, *my* wife is extraordinary." His eyes held an ardent flame.

I blushed. By and by, it struck me that he did not know I had banished Lady Catherine from the house, so I informed him.

"I am glad you ensured she could not harass you again. I shall pay her a visit next week. If she ever wishes to return, she must first give you an apology—one you deem adequate."

"Thank you."

"Please do not thank me." He brushed his knuckles over his

mouth. "I hate that I was not there to prevent her abuse. How can I ever make up for what I put you through? These past five days, I had every reason to believe you to be safe, yet I found each hour of our separation torturous. You did not know my fate, yet you carried on and looked after my sister. I never once fretted for Georgie, knowing she was with you."

"She comforted me as well."

"If you want, we shall go away to Pemberley, the seaside, the Lakes, or anywhere you name."

"When?"

"Monday or Tuesday."

"Do you mean the two of us or with Georgiana?"

"Either way, as you prefer."

What a tempting offer; I should love to go to the countryside or perhaps the seashore again! Yet my reverie did not last long. I could not disregard the possible consequences of the pretty notion. "This is not the best time for us to leave. We are still attempting to forge my reputation in town. And now, with your...disappearance and the ensuing gossip, we must remain to bolster yours."

"My foremost concern is you and what will make you happy."

One of us needed to be practical. I patted his forearm. "We shall stay until the spring, as planned."

"Are you certain?" Fitzwilliam cradled my cheek. "Will you be content to remain in London?"

"Yes. With a few exceptions, I have been treated better than expected. Besides, I have you and Georgiana, the amusements only London can offer, and my beloved aunt and uncle Gardiner nearby to boot, so how could I fail to be content?"

"Pray, do not grow *too* attached to the city." He pressed his lips to my forehead. "I am counting on you loving Pemberley as much as I do."

"No doubt I shall do so."

When we entered the house, Georgiana rushed from the front sitting room. She halted before us and raised both hands to her mouth. With a squeal, she ran into Fitzwilliam's arms. "Thank God, you are home at last!"

"It is wonderful to see you, dearest. I have missed you." Fitzwilliam removed one hand from Georgiana's back and laced his fingers through mine.

The sight beyond the entryway drew my notice: most of the servants had hied to the hall to welcome their master home. I spotted suspiciously shiny eyes on several of them, including Slade and Winston. The entire house came alive, humming with a palpable ambience of joy.

Sunday, 19 November
Darcy House

In the hazy first few seconds after I awoke, I lamented having to leave my wonderful dream—an idyllic depiction of Fitzwilliam's homecoming. But then I noted his arm around my waist and his warm presence at my back, and the events of yesterday returned to me. This time, my dream had resembled reality.

I turned to find him watching me and covered my mouth to yawn. "Good morning, my love."

"Good morning." He raised an eyebrow. "You slept well."

"How do you know?"

"You are usually up before me, and you tend to be a light sleeper. But I called your name several times in the last ten minutes. You smiled and carried on sleeping."

"Hmm. Well, I had a particularly pleasant dream in which my husband returned to me."

"It is obvious you needed the rest. I kept you up too late last night."

"Nay, there are a few things more important than sleep." Memories of our amorous activities the night before fostered my grin.

"Indeed." He moved on top of me and placed soft kisses on my face and down my neck.

As much as I revelled in his ministrations, bright rays of morning sunlight shone through the window, signalling the time as well past seven. I craved a more substantial form of exercise this morning, so I overcame my disinclination to interrupt him and patted his arse. "We had better get dressed."

He paused, and his eyes lifted to meet mine. "Must we?"

"My aunt and uncle Gardiner and Mrs. Stapleton will join us for breakfast, and I need a walk in the park to fortify myself for the callers I expect to receive today." Not to mention the dinner I should host tonight with the Fitzwilliams and the Townshends.

With an exaggerated sigh, he rolled onto his back and laid his arm over his forehead. "Very well, we shall walk."

I sat with my legs outstretched upon the sofa in the study whilst Fitzwilliam composed a letter he had deemed too important to put off until tomorrow. Our dinner guests had left, and Georgiana had retired. I blinked several times but could not seem to get through 'Lucy Gray', part of the volume of Wordsworth's *Lyrical Ballads* in my lap; the words kept fading into indistinct blots. Shifting my position, I straightened my spine.

The evening had gone well, except for the deafening rumpus Lady Catherine had made at the front door during the meal—her dissonant screeches had reached the dining room. Fitzwilliam had stood and clarified for those around the table that she would not be admitted until certain conditions had been met. Then he excused himself to inform Lady Catherine of his demands. The Townshends had the good graces to act heedless of the disturbance. The earl had displayed a look of chagrin, whilst Lord Berkeley grumbled his disapproval for our not allowing her entry. Lady Matlock, to her credit, told the viscount in a quiet yet firm voice to stay out of the matter.

Fitzwilliam stood from the seat at his desk and approached me.

I smiled at him. "Are you finished?"

"No, but I can see you are sleepy. Go on up to bed. I shall be there soon."

"But I..." I bit the inside of my cheek. I did not want to go to our chamber alone. The remembrance of the agonising mixture of despair, dread, and loneliness I had suffered there in his absence intruded upon my peace. But I ought not indulge such childish impulses. "You are right. I *am* weary."

Fitzwilliam lifted my book and placed it on the table. He took my hand, helped me to my feet, and left a lingering kiss on my lips.

I left the study and reached the second-floor landing when my gait slowed; an elusive concept tarried at the verge of my memory. *Mrs. Winters's prediction!* I had not passed on the warning to Fitzwilliam. I spun round and returned to the study, entering the well-lit room to find no sign of my husband. Where had he gone?

The door to the garden had been left ajar. As I drew nearer, I could make out voices. Fitzwilliam argued with another man out on the stone path. With each step I took, the severity of their altercation grew more distinct. The stranger used harsh, malevolent tones. A chill coursed down my back.

"I understand how difficult this has been for you." Fitzwilliam maintained a calm demeanour. "And I have done everything in my power to mitigate the damage to your reputation."

"Do you expect me to be grateful that you took steps to lessen the harm *you* had wrought?"

I passed through the door, and the man's features became visible in the moonlight: *Mr. Cecil Haddington*. His speech, distorted by anger and hatred, bore no resemblance to the mild voice I associated with him. I should never have deemed him capable of such animosity, such venom. I moved towards them.

"Your friends think you are selfless and generous for condescending to help me, but you are nothing but a fraud!" Mr. Haddington's left arm whipped to and fro, emphasising his words. "In actuality, my father would still be alive if not for you. It is *your* fault I lost my title, my estate, and my reputation. You have pretended to be a friend, but you are more of a traitor than my father ever was!"

"I *am* your friend. I had no choice but to report what Lord Carswell had done. You must see that."

"Of course you had a choice! You could have confronted my father and allowed him to promise he would never again sell information he learnt from my uncle with no one the wiser. Instead, you ensured my family's ruin, and I lost the only woman I have ever loved."

Mr. Haddington held a shiny object in his right hand—a pistol, pointed at Fitzwilliam! I glanced over my shoulder towards the study. Should I go back? I could ring for Slade, call out to Martin in the hall, or search for the pistol my husband kept in his desk. But I could not risk leaving now when Fitzwilliam could be shot at any moment. I could not lose him! I must find a way to stop Mr. Haddington.

"Believe me, I am truly sorry for that. I had been unaware of your courtship of Miss Weston until after the family left town. If I had known, I should have pleaded your case with Mr. Weston."

"It would not have made a difference, and your sympathy does nothing for me." Mr. Haddington spat upon the ground. "But my revenge is at hand. I shall take pleasure in taking your life."

"You cannot expect to get away with this. My servants will hear the shot."

"I have considered that. I shall leave the gun by your hand so it appears to be a suicide, then hide in the bushes until your servants find you. Once that happens, they will be focused upon you. I shall be able to slip out unseen. Of course, I shall ensure the wound is fatal." Mr. Haddington stepped closer to Fitzwilliam.

No, I will not let this happen! They had not noticed me yet, and my slippers made no noise upon the smooth path. How could I deter

Mr. Haddington from his course? Perhaps I could persuade him to listen to reason or...convince him that I sympathised with him. I continued towards them.

"You do not want to do this, Haddington."

"On the contrary, I have been in anticipation of this moment."

Fitzwilliam saw me and flinched. He raised his hand to halt me. "Elizabeth, go back in the house!" He hissed the words. I pressed onwards.

"Mrs. Darcy!" Mr. Haddington jerked to the side and pointed the gun at me.

I stood still, my eyes locked on the pistol. Surely, he would not shoot me!

"This is the last thing I wanted." Mr. Haddington shook his head. "But now that you are here, I must insist you stay."

My husband inched towards me, all outward pretence of his former composure gone. "Haddington, you must let her go! She has naught to do with this. Your grudge is with me alone."

"That is far enough, Darcy. Do not move again, or I shall shoot." Haddington aimed the pistol towards my husband's chest. "I shall not kill her. Before I leave, I shall knock her unconscious—that way, when she accuses me, her head injury will ensure her word is doubted."

"If you so much as touch her, I will—"

"Enough!" I held my palm out to Fitzwilliam and strove for a scornful tenor. "You have had your say."

"Elizabeth, please—"

"Be quiet. It is *my* turn to speak now." I sent him an intent look—a silent plea for him to cooperate—then regarded Mr. Haddington, softening my expression. "I overheard enough of your conversation to understand why you want revenge. I am not here to plead for my husband's life. Nevertheless, I think...um..." a figure moving in the shrubbery caught my eye. Could it be one of the servants? I cleared my throat. "It occurs to me that killing my husband is not the best solution. It is far too risky for you, and any satisfaction will be short-lived."

"This is most peculiar, coming from you." Mr. Haddington blinked at me. "Am I to understand you have a better suggestion?"

"Yes, a far more effective one. My husband is a proud man, and he is covetous of me. Nothing would hurt him more than if I spent the night with another man." I gave Mr. Haddington the best coquettish smile I could muster.

"This is madness, Elizabeth!" Fitzwilliam's eyes flashed.

Mr. Haddington's head edged sideways, and the silvery moonbeams lent his eyes a maniacal cast. "Well now, that is a *fascinating* notion. But why would you be willing to do this? I should have sworn you and Darcy had made a love match."

"I had thought so too." My heart thundered. Did I sound angry enough to make my offer seem credible? "But I have learnt that since our arrival in town, he has been cavorting with Miss Frances Comerford." The man on the garden path crept closer, and his features became visible: *Mr. Dennis*.

"Ah, then that particular rumour was true. Your offer is tempting, but I cannot agree to it. If I allowed Darcy to live, he would tell the Alien Office everything I have done. I should be hanged."

"No, you may be assured he would not say a word. The last thing he would want is for everyone to find out he is a cuckold."

"Elizabeth, please..." Fitzwilliam's attention veered for a moment to a spot beyond Mr. Haddington's right shoulder, where Mr. Dennis approached. "You cannot do this."

"Hush, Fitzwilliam!" I raised my voice with the hope of concealing any sounds Mr. Dennis might make. "This is between Mr. Haddington and me. You have no say in the matter."

Mr. Haddington rubbed the back of his neck. He studied me as though to gauge my verity. At length, he grinned. "Darcy was a fool to betray you. I think your proposal is clever. It will be a far greater punishment for him to live with the knowledge of your infidelity." He narrowed his eyes at Fitzwilliam. "Do not try to prevent us from leaving, or I shall be compelled to shoot you."

I glanced at my husband. "Tell Mr. Haddington you will not stop us."

Fitzwilliam released a heavy breath. "I...shall not stop you."

"Shall we go?" Mr. Haddington held his free hand out to me.

"By all means." I took two steps towards Mr. Haddington and halted. "Oh, but please put the pistol away. I am deathly afraid of firearms."

With a slow nod, Mr. Haddington put the weapon in the pocket of his coat. Mr. Dennis sprang forwards and flung himself at Mr. Haddington, toppling him to the ground.

Fitzwilliam ran to me, threw his arm around my waist, and rushed me back to the study. He held me in a gentle rocking motion. "Thank God you are safe. You should not have taken such a risk. He might have killed you!"

"I could not stand by and allow you to be shot." A succession of trembles beset me. If I had arrived at the study any later, I may have lost him. I whimpered against his cravat.

"All is well, my love." He glanced over my shoulder. "Dennis has Haddington in handcuffs."

"Thank goodness for that. Did you expect Mr. Dennis tonight?"

"No, I cannot account for his fortuitous appearance."

We remained locked in each other's arms with Fitzwilliam rubbing my back until I calmed.

When Mr. Dennis knocked on the study door half an hour later, Fitzwilliam and I sat on the sofa with glasses of brandy.

My husband let Mr. Dennis in and shook his hand. "Where is Haddington?"

"Your grooms are guarding him in the carriage-house. He gave me a full confession."

"Thank you. Your arrival is as appreciated as it was unexpected."

I stood. "I wish to add my heartfelt thanks, Mr. Dennis, for your timely intervention."

A reddish hue darkened Mr. Dennis's ears. "You are both most welcome."

My husband gave Mr. Dennis a glass of the liquor and directed him to a nearby chair before sitting beside me on the sofa. "How did you know to come here tonight?"

Mr. Dennis reclined in the chair and took a sip of brandy. "I had spoken to Ernest Haddington at length during the investigation of Lord Carswell, and he blamed no one more than himself for their arrest and prosecution. I could not understand why he would plan to have you or anyone else killed for retribution. I wondered if a component of this investigation had been overlooked.

"So I reviewed the evidence and investigative notes we had collected. When I examined Mr. Ernest Haddington's suicide note and the message sent to Eli Leeson, I found the handwriting in both contained inconsistencies when compared to the former colonel's earlier written statement. I deduced the notes had been written to mimic his handwriting, and Cecil Haddington was the most obvious suspect. If he had known of Darcy's involvement in his father's arrest for treason, he would have had a motive to hire the assassin. Since the two of you left the Alien Office yesterday, I have watched Mr. Haddington's movements and followed him here tonight."

Mr. Dennis guzzled the remaining liquor and set the glass on the table. "Even though I am aware of the pertinent facts in this instance, I should like you to answer a few questions for my report."

"Yes, of course." Fitzwilliam refilled Mr. Dennis's glass. "But I imagine my wife is exhausted." He placed his hand on mine. "Elizabeth, you ought to go on upstairs."

"I am not the least bit tired any longer."

After a moment's hesitation, he nodded. "As you wish."

I caught Mr. Dennis's fleeting smirk as he removed a small notebook and a pencil from his coat pocket. He faced my husband. "When did you first see Mr. Haddington this evening?"

"It must have been close to midnight. I had been at my desk writing a letter when Haddington knocked on the door to the garden. He asked me to come out and speak to him."

"Were you in the study alone?"

Fitzwilliam glanced at me. "Yes. Elizabeth had just gone up to bed, or so I thought."

Mr. Dennis wrote in his notebook. "Did Haddington explain why he did not go to the front door?"

"He maintained he had been unable to sleep and took a walk. He said he went through the mews into the back garden on the chance he might find me in the study."

"What happened next?"

"I expressed my condolences for his uncle's death. For a minute or so, we had an unremarkable conversation. Then he looked around us, presumably to ensure we were alone, and pulled out a pistol. He declared his intent to kill me. He blamed me for the loss of his reputation. He admitted to having hired Eli Leeson and killing his uncle, whom he also held culpable for his woes." Fitzwilliam scowled. "He appeared to have no remorse for the murder."

"Why do you think he wanted you out in the garden?"

"I suppose because my nearest servant was stationed in the hall, whereas most of the others would have been asleep." Fitzwilliam turned to me. "Why did you return to the study?"

"It occurred to me that I had forgotten to relate a warning from Mrs. Winters." I shared a quick look with Mr. Dennis. "She is a Romani lady who came to see me on Friday." I mentioned the assault that had led to Fitzwilliam rescuing her young daughter.

My husband frowned. "Yes, I recall what happened that day."

I recounted Mrs. Winters's declaration of having seen him in a vision.

Fitzwilliam's brows shot up. "She gave you an accurate portrayal of my circumstances."

"She asked me to warn you that someone you trusted would betray you."

"That is...interesting."

Mr. Dennis shook his head. "You cannot put credence in anything said by a fortune-teller. Besides, her statements are too general to have any real significance." He gulped the rest of the brandy. "I bet Mrs. Winters repeats similar predictions to everyone. Most of us will be disappointed by a friend sooner or later."

"As I told Mrs. Winters, I do not believe in fortune-telling." I angled my head towards Fitzwilliam. "Nevertheless, she provided assurance when I most needed it, and I do not doubt she wanted to help us. Maybe she has an authentic gift."

"In any case, I trust your instincts." Fitzwilliam raised his glass to me. "To Mrs. Winters."

My glass clinked against his. "To Mrs. Winters."

Mr. Dennis closed his notebook. "Mrs. Darcy, I commend your masterful treatment of Mr. Haddington tonight. I doubt any of the women who have worked for the agency over the years could have done better."

"In truth, I was terrified he would see through my ruse."

"Yet you carried on despite your fear and resolved the immediate danger. If you ever wish to serve your country, you may count upon my recommendation. The Alien Office would be fortunate to have you."

I beamed at Fitzwilliam, who gave me a pained look. He glared at Mr. Dennis. "You forget yourself. I cannot believe you made such an irresponsible suggestion. I absolutely forbid..." He coughed. "What I mean to say is...my wife could not possibly..."

I touched Fitzwilliam's arm. "Thank you for the compliment, Mr. Dennis. It is rare for a lady to be offered such an opportunity, but I shall decline. I believe my husband and I have had enough dramatic adventures to last us a lifetime."

"Of course, I understand." Mr. Dennis stood and took his leave of us.

Fitzwilliam locked the garden door after him and returned to me. "It is high time I took you to bed."

"But you did not finish your letter."

"It can wait."

My smile took on a teasing arch. "And I already told you I am no longer sleepy."

"Yes, I know." His lips claimed mine in a deep, hungry kiss.

When he withdrew, I leaned upon him and mewled softly against his neck. My feet sailed off the floor as he scooped me into his arms. He nuzzled my throat, prompting me to giggle, and carried me out of the study door towards the stairs.

My faith in him had endured despite every attempt made to quash it, raise doubts, or undermine me. The darling man was mine, now and forevermore.

The End

Note to Readers

Thank you so much for reading *The Mysterious Disappearance of Mr. Darcy*! I hope you enjoyed it, and I would greatly appreciate an honest review or rating at Amazon and/or Goodreads.

About the Author

KELLY MILLER

Award-winning author Kelly Miller is a native Californian and Anglophile, who made her first visit to England in 2019. When not pondering a plot point or turn of phrase, she can be found playing the piano, singing, or walking her dogs. Kelly resides in Silicon Valley with her husband and their pets.

The Mysterious Disappearance of Mr. Darcy, a *Pride and Prejudice* Regency romantic mystery, is her ninth published book. The first eight are:

Death Takes a Holiday at Pemberley, *a* Pride and Prejudice *Regency romantic variation with a touch of fantasy. Winner: Royal Dragonfly Book Awards and Indies Today Book Awards; Finalist: International Book Awards and Book Excellence Awards*

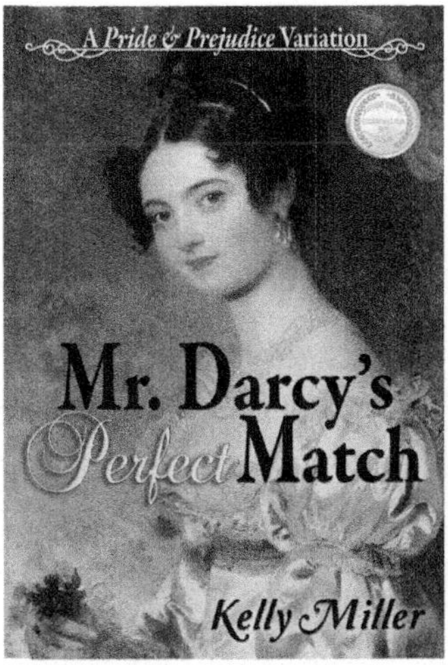

Mr. Darcy's Perfect Match, *a* Pride and Prejudice *Regency romantic variation. Recommended Read: Author Shout Reader Ready Awards*

Accusing Mr. Darcy, a Pride and Prejudice *Regency romantic mystery. Winner: Firebird Book Awards and Queer Indie Awards-Ally Division; Recommended Read: Author Shout Reader Ready Awards; Finalist: Wishing Shelf Book Awards and Chanticleer International Book Awards*

A Consuming Love, a Pride and Prejudice *Regency romantic novella. Winner: Royal Dragonfly Book Awards; Recommended Read: Author Shout Reader Ready Awards*

Captive Hearts, a Persuasion *Regency romantic variation. Winner: Royal Dragonfly Book Awards and Incipere Awards; Top Pick: Author Shout Reader Ready Awards; Red Ribbon Winner: Wishing Shelf Book Awards; Finalist: Chanticleer International Book Awards; Runner-Up: Indies Today Book Awards*

A Dutiful Son, *a* Pride and Prejudice *Regency romantic variation, an Amazon #1 Best Seller; Bronze medal winner, Readers' Favorite Book Awards.*

The Darcy Secret, *a* Pride and Prejudice *Regency romantic variation, an Amazon #1 Best Seller.*

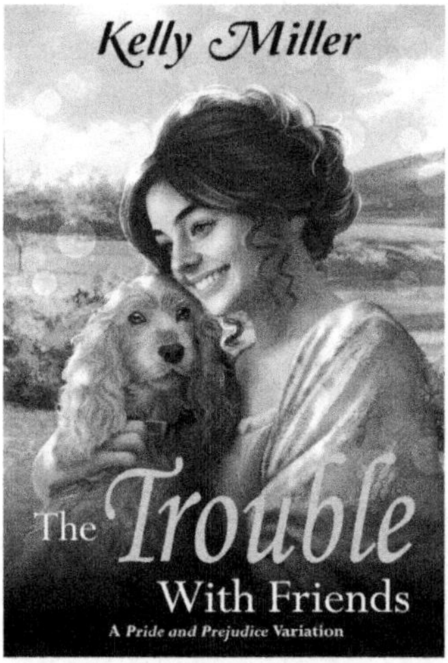

The Trouble With Friends, *a* Pride and Prejudice *Regency romantic variation, an Amazon #1 Best Seller.*

Where to Find Kelly

X / Twitter: @Kellyrei007

https://twitter.com/Kellyrei007

Facebook: https://www.facebook.com/Author.Kelly.Miller

Instagram: @kelly.miller.author

https://www.instagram.com/kelly.miller.author/

Threads: @kelly.miller.author

https://www.threads.net/@kelly.miller.author

TikTok: kellymillerauthor

https://www.tiktok.com/@kellymillerauthor

BlueSky: @kellymiller.bsky.social

https://bsky.app/profile/kellymiller.bsky.social

Goodreads:

https://www.goodreads.com/author/show/19251479.Kelly_Miller

BookBub: https://www.bookbub.com/profile/kelly-miller-5fb23fbe-af73-4174-923c-8130e1af8779

Meryton Press Blog Page: www.kellymiller.merytonpress.com

Acknowledgements

In a woefully short lifespan, Jane Austen created a host of unforgettable characters that continue to live on in films, books, and plays all over the world. I am most grateful to her.

I appreciate the opportunity to work with my wonderful editors, Carol S. Bowes and Jo Abbott. Both ladies brought out the best in my writing and shared their valuable Regency knowledge. Jo's familiarity with British English helped me keep Americanisms out of my story. A tremendous thank you to Pemberley Darcy for creating the gorgeous cover for this book. I am grateful to Suzanne Minae for formatting my manuscript and giving it a professional appearance. Finally, thank you to Tim for being my first reader.

Printed in Great Britain
by Amazon

42206900R00121